P9-AFS-530

# *FUN* WITH PCR

# 實用漢語課本

## 寫聽練習

## I

## (Traditional Characters)

*Peggy Wang*

1996

To my daughters Linda & Vivian:

Learning Chinese can be FUN!

ISBN 0-9697499-2-9

Copyright © 1994 by EALS
All rights reserved.
This book may not be reproduced, in whole
or in part, in any form without the written
permission from the publisher.

# CONTENTS

VOCABULARY LIST

MEASURE WORDS CHART

RADICALS CHART

ENGLISH-CHINESE GLOSSARY (PCR I & II)

# INTRODUCTION

FUN WITH PCR is designed specifically to accompany the widely adopted Chinese textbooks - PRACTICAL CHINESE READER I & II (實用漢語課本, The Commercial Press, Beijing).

OBJECTIVES:
* To provide students with a variety of interesting and challenging exercises, with topics relating particularly to the daily lives of North American students;
* To supplement the original textbooks with more practical vocabulary and key structures whenever needed (Ex: 會 and 可以 appear in very early exercises.);
* To familiarize students with both types of characters -  traditional & simplified.

AURAL EXERCISES:
* Dictation (Pinyin; tones; characters);
* Differentiation of words with similar pronunciations;
* Chinese - English translations;
* Questions & Answers;
* Filling in the blanks with missing key words;
* Listening comprehension (True or False; Multiple choice;  Missing information).

WRITTEN EXERCISES:
* Character practicing & Word formation;
* Crossword puzzle (Pinyin & character);
* Matching (Question with answer; Subject with predicate);
* Riddles and Tongue twisters;
* Guided English-Chinese translations: To translate following the illustrated pattern;
* Questions & Answers (Chinese etiquette, etc.)
* Guided composition (Word order & Sentence order)
* Task - oriented composition (Leave a message; Rent a room; Plan a trip; Comments on some controversial social issues, etc.)
* Mind Stretchers (To learn Chinese through reasoning and logical thinking)
* Reading comprehension (Anecdote; Moral stories, etc.).

Comments and suggestions to improve this workbook would be  appreciated.
Special thanks to my colleagues at UCDavis - Dr.Tim Xie and Mrs. Loretta Gibbs for their constant support and encouragement，to Robert Michell for his enthusiasm and his hawk-eyed proofreading of this text.

Peggy Wang
UCDavis, CA, USA,    June, 1993

# THE PINYIN SYSTEM

## *PRONUNCIATION EXERCISES*

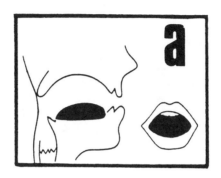

元音 Vowels
a o e i u ü

辅音 Consonants
b d g z zh j
p t k c ch q
m n h s sh x
f l r

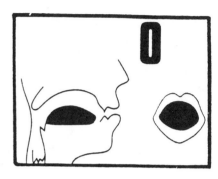

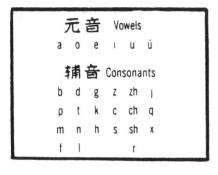

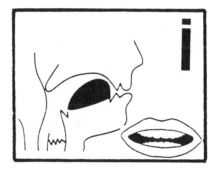

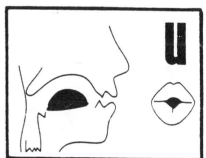

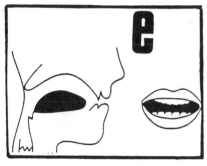

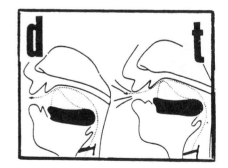

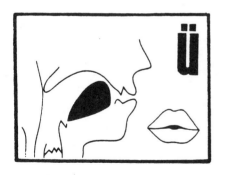

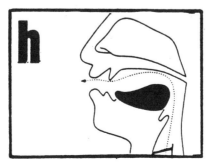

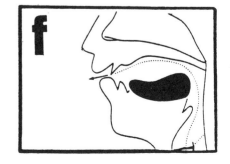

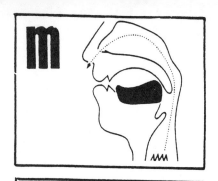

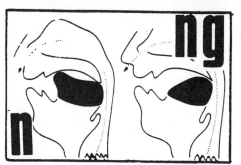

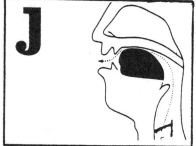

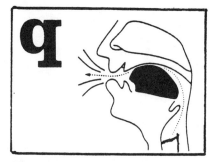

X ≠ English 'c'

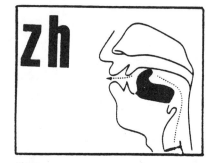

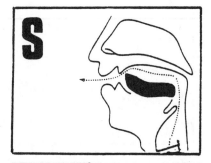

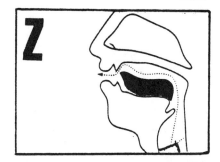

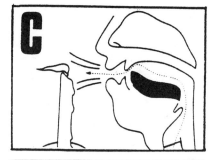

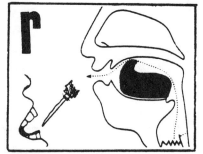

er (·r)

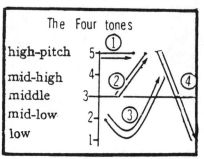

| Compound Vowels | | | |
|---|---|---|---|
| a: | ai | ao | |
| o: | ou | | |
| e: | ei | | |
| i: | ia | ie· | iao |
| u: | ua | uo | uai | uei |
| ü: | üe | | |

### Vowels plus Nasal Consonants

| | | | | |
|---|---|---|---|---|
| an | en | ang | eng | ong |
| ian | in | iang | ing | iong |
| uan | uen | uang | ueng | |
| üan | ün | | | |

### The Construction of a Chinese Syllable

| Single vowel | è  à  ŏ |
|---|---|
| Compound vowel | + tone | ài  ǎo |
| Consonant and vowel | hē  ēn |
| | zhōng  xué |

### The Four tones

high-pitch 5
mid-high 4
middle 3
mid-low 2
low 1

① ② ③ ④

-4-

## PRACTICE THE FOLLOWING TONES:

The second tone and the fourth tone:

| | | | | |
|---|---|---|---|---|
| á | á | à | à | |
| ú | ú | ù | ù | |
| bá | bá | bà | bà | |
| | bá | bà | bá | bà |
| dá | dá | dà | dà | |
| | dá | dà | dá | dà |
| bó | bó | bò | bò | |
| | bó | bò | bó | bò |
| gé | gé | gè | gè | |
| | gé | gè | gé | gè |
| bí | bí | bì | bì | |
| | bí | bì | bí | bì |
| dí | dí | dì | dì | di |
| | dí | dì | dí | dì |
| bú | bú | bù | bù | |
| | bú | bù | bú | bù |
| dú | dú | dù | dù | |
| | dú | dù | dú | dù |

The first tone and the third tone:

| | | | | | |
|---|---|---|---|---|---|
| pāo | pāo | pǎo | pǎo | pāo | pǎo |
| kān | kān | kǎn | kǎn | kān | kǎn |
| bāng | bāng | bǎng | bǎng | bāng | bǎng |
| nī | nī | nǐ | nǐ | nī | nǐ |
| hāo | hāo | hǎo | hǎo | hāo | hǎo |
| tā | tā | tǎ | tǎ | tā | tǎ |

## PRACTICE THE FOLLOWING COMPOUND VOWELS:

| | | |
|---|---|---|
| a | i | ai |
| a | o | ao |
| o | u | ou |
| e | i | ei |
| i | a | ia (ya) |
| i | e | ie (ye) |
| i | ao | iao (yao) |
| i | ou | iu (you) |
| u | a | ua (wa) |
| u | o | uo (wo) |
| u | ai | uai (wai) |
| u | ei | ui (wei) |
| ü | e | üe (yue ) |

## PRACTICE THE FOLLOWING VOWELS WITH A NASAL CONSONANT:
Pay attention to the difference between -n and -ng.

| | | | |
|---|---|---|---|
| an | an | ang | ang |
| en | en | eng | eng |
| an | en | ang | eng |
| in | in (yin) | ing | ing (ying) |
| uen | uen (wen) | ueng | ueng (weng) |
| uen | uen | ong | ong (wong) |
| in | uen | ing | ueng (weng) |
| ün | ün(yun) | iong | iong (yong) |
| uen | ün | ueng | iong |
| an | ang | ong | |
| ian (yan) | iang (yang) | iong (yong) | |
| uan (wan) | uang (wang) | uong (wong) | |

-6-

# THE IMPORTANCE OF TONES

# THE CHANGE OF TONES

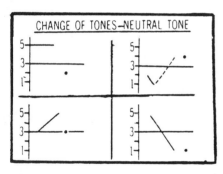

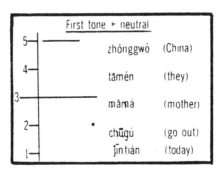

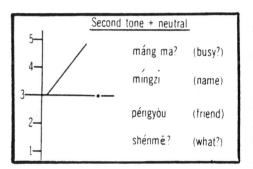

**CHANGE OF TONES—NEUTRAL TONE**

**First tone + neutral**

| | |
|---|---|
| zhōngguó | (China) |
| tāmén | (they) |
| māma | (mother) |
| chūqú | (go out) |
| jīntiān | (today) |

**Second tone + neutral**

| | |
|---|---|
| máng ma? | (busy?) |
| míngzi | (name) |
| péngyǒu | (friend) |
| shénme? | (what?) |

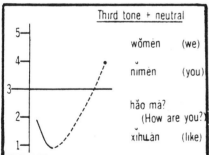

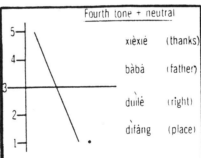

**Third tone + neutral**

| | |
|---|---|
| wǒmen | (we) |
| nǐmen | (you) |
| hǎo ma? | (How are you?) |
| xǐhuan | (like) |

**Fourth tone + neutral**

| | |
|---|---|
| xièxie | (thanks) |
| bàba | (father) |
| duìle | (right) |
| dìfāng | (place) |

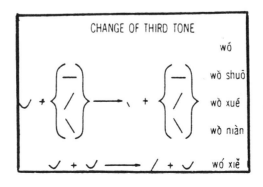

**CHANGE OF THIRD TONE**

| | |
|---|---|
| | wó |
| | wǒ shuō |
| | wǒ xué |
| | wǒ niàn |
| | wó xiě |

# MEMORIZATION

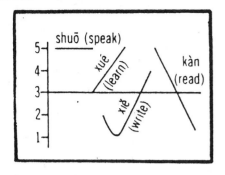

shuō zhōngwén!

xué zhōngwén

xiě zhōngwén

kàn zhōngwén

zàijiàn!

wǒ

wǒmen

nǐ

nǐmen

tā

tāmen

zǎo qǐ chuáng

Zǎochen zuò zǎocāo

ZǍO QǏCHUÁNG,
ZǍO·CHÉN ZUÒ ZǍOCĀO,

ZUÒ ZǍOCĀO.

ZUÒCĀO SHĒNTǏ HǍO.

# LESSONS 1,2,3

1. Circle the right sound:

   1) a    i    o    u    e          6) wan   wang   wen   weng

   2) an    ao    ang               7) yi    yin    ying

   3) wo    ou                      8) bi    bin    bing

   4) e    en    eng                9) mang   tang   dang

   5) wa    wu    wo    wei        10) ye    lie    nie

2. Circle the right tone:

   1) ā    á    ǎ    à             6) āng   áng   ǎng   àng

   2) bī    bí    bǐ    bì          7) kāng   kán   kǎn   kàn

   3) pāo    páo    pǎo    pào      8) māo   máo   mǎo   mào

   4) dēng    déng    děng    dèng  9) nē    né    ně    nè

   5) gē    gé    gě    gè         10) hōu   hóu   hǒu   hòu

3. Mark the correct tone on the following syllables:

   1) bao          6) pa          11) mao

   2) hao          7) bo          12) kan

   3) he           8) ni          13) li

   4) guo          9) gu          14) kuo

   5) kan         10) lan         15) bie

4. Choose the correct one:

   1) mō    māo     6) gě    kě     11) bù    pù

   2) gùo    kuò    7) bǎng   pǎng  12) dǎ    tà

   3) biē    piē    8) bù    pù     13) kǒu   gǒu

   4) hé    hén     9) tōu    dōu   14) lǎn   nán

   5) dì    tì     10) hěn    kěn   15) hǔ    gǔ

5. Circle the neutral tone: Note the neutral tone is not used in every case.

1) women　　　　6) dou hao　　　　11) mama

2) ni mang　　　7) tamen　　　　　12) hen hao

3) mang ma　　　8) nimen　　　　　13) hao ma

4) wo hao　　　 9) ni ne　　　　　14) Gubo

5) gege　　　　　10) hen mang　　　 15) didi

6. Listen to the following dialogues and check the statements as right ( ✓ ) or wrong ( X ):

1 ) (　) The man has one brother.
　　(　) The man is busy.

2 ) (　) The man's younger brothers are all well.
　　(　) Some of them are busy.

3 ) (　) The man's brothers are all well.
　　(　) The man is also very busy.

4 ) (　) None of them are busy.
　　(　) None of us are busy either.

5 ) (　) The man is busy.
　　(　) The women is also busy.

6 ) (　) Four people are all well.
　　(　) Three of them are male.

7. Practice the following characters.

| | |
|---|---|
| 你 | 弟 |
| 好 | 都 |
| 我 | 他 |
| 很 | 們 |
| 不 | 嗎 |
| 呢 | 忙 |
| 哥 | 也 |

Find from above the characters which share the same initial stroke as the ones given below. Note that a stroke may vary in length.

哥 :                                    你:

呢:

8. MAKE SENTENCE : Make a sentence, using the words given:

很好
你嗎好

很他忙嗎

哥哥
弟弟
我我
很都
忙

都我們
也忙很

9. Fill in the blanks:

<u>with 嗎、呢</u>

1) 他哥哥忙，他弟弟也忙＿＿＿？
2) 他哥哥很好，他弟弟＿＿＿？
3) 我們都很忙，你們＿＿＿？
4) 他們都不忙，你們也都不忙＿＿＿？
5) 我弟弟不好，你弟弟＿＿＿？
6) 你們都好，他們＿＿＿？

<u>with 都不、不都、也都、也、都、都不很</u>

1) 你忙，我＿＿＿忙，我們＿＿＿忙。
2) 他們都很忙，你們 ＿＿＿＿＿＿ 很忙嗎？
3) 我忙，他不忙。我們＿＿＿＿＿＿忙。
4) 哥哥不忙，弟弟也不忙，他們＿＿＿＿＿＿忙。
5) 哥哥不很好，弟弟也不很好。他們＿＿＿＿＿＿好。

10. WORD ORDER & SENTENCE ORDER:

Rearrange the words in each entry to make a grammatical sentence.

Rearrange the sentences to make a meaningful passage.

1) A) 也 忙 很 哥哥 我

B) 都 忙 很 他們

C) 忙 很 我 弟弟

The correct sentence order:＿＿＿＿＿＿＿

2) A) 好 他們 都 不很

B) 弟弟 他 好 不很 也

C) 哥哥 他 好 不很

The correct sentence order:＿＿＿＿＿＿＿

11. TRANSLATION: Translate the following sentences into Chinese (characters), using the illustrated patterns.

NOTES ON GRAMMAR: Any of the adverbs 也，都，很，不 may be used by alone or in combination with the others. 也，都，很 appear in the sequence as shown below. 不 may appear either before or after 都 and 很. The variations of the word order will give different meanings.

> Ex: 都不 (all not - none of ); 不都 (not all);
> 不很 (not very);　　　　很不 (really not)

A stative verb (SV) is an adjective used as a verb in a sentence, such as 好 (being good).

A stative verb functions like a verb and 是 (to be) is not needed as is in English.

S + ( 也 )( 都 )( 很 ) + SV + ( 嗎 )
=====================
他們　　　都 很 忙。_____They are all very busy.

_____Are you all very busy too?

_____The elder brother is nice.

_____Is the younger brother also nice?

S + ( 也 )( 不 ) 都 ( 不 ) + SV + ( 嗎 )
=====================
我們　　　不 都　　　忙。___Not all of us are busy.

_____None of us are busy.

_____Not all of them are nice.

_____None of them are nice either.

_____Are they all busy as well?

## 12. SEEK & FIND:

Try to find as many sentences or questions as possible from the following jumble of characters.
Look horizontally, vertically and diagonally.
Circle each sentence or question and copy them.

| 他 | 你 | 好 | 嗎 | 你 | 們 | 好 | 他 |
|---|---|---|---|---|---|---|---|
| 我 | 我 | 們 | 都 | 忙 | 嗎 | 都 | 不 |
| 他 | 們 | 不 | 忙 | 嗎 | 哥 | 哥 | 好 |
| 弟 | 弟 | 很 | 好 | 哥 | 哥 | 呢 | 你 |
| 弟 | 弟 | 忙 | 哥 | 哥 | 也 | 忙 | 們 |
| 他 | 好 | 嗎 | 忙 | 好 | 忙 | 呢 | 也 |
| 你 | 們 | 也 | 都 | 很 | 好 | 嗎 | 好 |

我不好。

你忙.　　我不忙.

我們不都忙.

-14-

# LESSONS 4,5,6

1. Circle the right one:

|  | | | | |  | | | | |
|---|---|---|---|---|---|---|---|---|---|
| 1) | zhē | zhé | zhě | zhè | 8) | dāi | dái | dǎi | dài |
| 2) | chē | ché | chě | chè | 9) | shū | shú | shǔ | shù |
| 3) | bū | bú | bǔ | bù | 10) | gūo | gúo | gǔo | gùo |
| 4) | shī | shí | shǐ | shì | 11) | fū | fú | fǔ | fù |
| 5) | bā | bá | bǎ | bà | 12) | rēn | rén | rěn | rèn |
| 6) | hān | hán | hǎn | hàn | 13) | zhōng | zhóng | zhǒng | zhòng |
| 7) | yū | yú | yǔ | yù | 14) | lāo | láo | lǎo | lào |

2. Add the correct tone marks to the following disyllabic words or phrases:

| | | | | | |
|---|---|---|---|---|---|
| 1) | zhongwen | 11) | gangbi | 21) | luyin |
| 2) | zaijian | 12) | qianbi | 22) | wenti |
| 3) | tan tan | 13) | gongzuo | 23) | zidian |
| 4) | jianada | 14) | guojia | 24) | dianhua |
| 5) | kan shu | 15) | huida | 25) | wansui |
| 6) | wen wo | 16) | xiexie | 26) | hanzi |
| 7) | yingguo | 17) | chuantong | 27) | pengyou |
| 8) | fayin | 18) | geming | 28) | daifu |
| 9) | gongyuan | 19) | liuli | 29) | baozhi |
| 10) | fangfa | 20) | diandeng | 30) | laoshi |

3. Discriminate the half third tone from the fourth tone by circling the half third tone:

| | | | | | |
|---|---|---|---|---|---|
| 1) | (hao)kan | hao kan | 4) | fangwen | fang wen |
| 2) | youming | youming | 5) | mama | ma ma |
| 3) | kan shu | kan shu | 6) | yanjing | yanjing |

4. Choose the correct one:

1) bĕi    pĕi          6) rào    shào        11) rōng    réng

2) dàng   dèng         7) gái    kăi         12) bào     păo

3) zhī chī shī rī      8) sháo   shŏu        13) lū      lŭ

4) liú    lóu          9) bĭ     pí          14) zhăi    chái

5) shĕ    shĭ          10) zhè ché shè rē    15) chòu    shōu

5. Listen and circle the appropriate illustration:

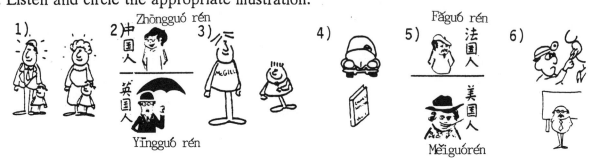

6. Listen to the conversation and check the statements as right (V) or wrong(X):

1) (   ) This Chinese book belongs to the man.
   (   ) The man has a Chinese friend.

2) (   ) The man is studying Chinese.
   (   ) His Chinese teacher is from China and is very nice.

3) (   ) The American car is good.          (Mĕiguó:America)
   (   ) Not all Japanese cars are good.    (Rìbĕn:Japan)

4) (   ) The man's father is a teacher.
   (   ) The man's mother is a doctor.

5) (   ) The man's elder brother is busy.
   (   ) The brother's friend is also busy.

6) (   ) The man's doctor is Dr.Lee.
   (   ) Dr.Lee is also the woman's doctor.

7. Practice the following characters:

| 這 | 你 | 書 | 中 |
|---|---|---|---|
| 是 | 她 | 漢 | 美 |
| 爸 | 那 | 語 | |
| 誰 | 大 | 老 | |
| 媽 | 夫 | 師 | |
| 朋 | 的 | 哪 | |
| 友 | 車 | 國 | |

Find from the above the characters which share the same initial stroke as the ones given below. Include also characters from the previous lessons.
Note that a stroke may vary in length.

語:

師:

的:

大:

媽:

8. Write a sentence, using the words given.

 是國那哪

 誰是你

 爸爸媽媽的是　這車

 是人國你哪

9. Fill in the blanks with 也，都，那，哪，的，誰，車
1) 我哥哥，弟弟＿＿很忙。
2) 她是＿＿國人？
3) ＿＿是美國 (America) 人？
4) 我媽媽的＿＿是日本 (Japanese) 車。
5) 你很好，他＿＿很好嗎？
6) ＿＿是你們＿＿老師嗎？

10. WORD ORDER & SENTENCE ORDER:
Rearrange the words in each entry to make a grammatical sentence, then arrange the sentenced to a logical order to make a meaningful passage.

1) A) 都　美國　車　好　不

B) 是　那　的　車　我大夫

C) 車　都　美國　的　他們　是　車

D) 這　我哥哥　是　的　車

The correct sentence order: ＿＿＿＿＿＿＿

-18-

2)A) 朋友 好 的 我爸爸 是 也 她

 B) 漢語 是 中國人 老師 的 我們
 (Zhōngguórén)

 C) 我們 漢語 老師 的 那 是

 D) 哪國 人 老師 漢語 是 的 你們

 E) 誰 那 是

The correct sentence order: _____

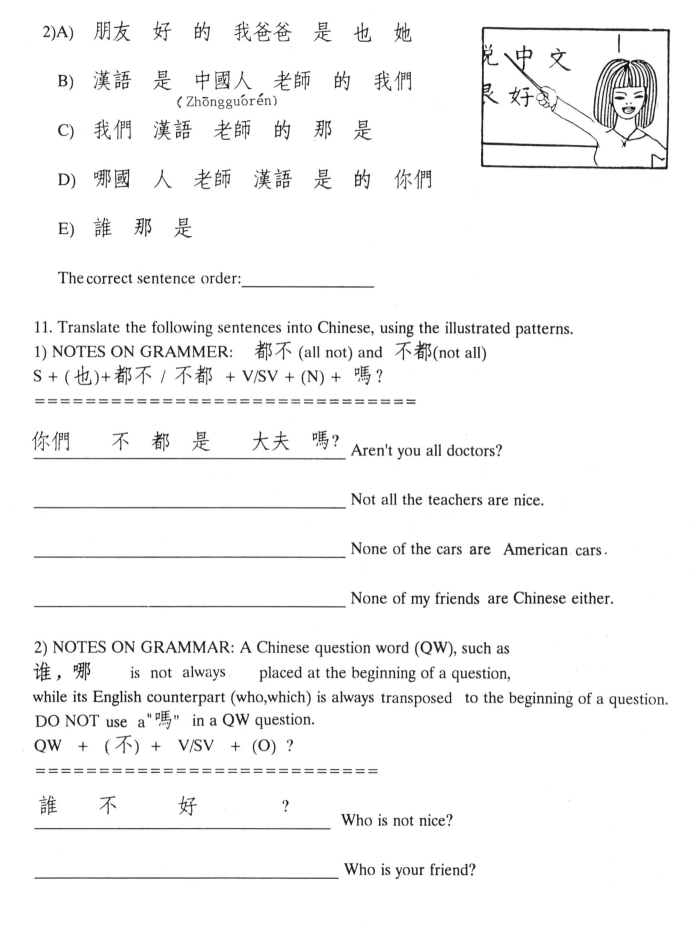

11. Translate the following sentences into Chinese, using the illustrated patterns.
1) NOTES ON GRAMMER:  都不 (all not) and 不都(not all)
S + ( 也)+都不 / 不都 + V/SV + (N) + 嗎？
============================

你們　不　都　是　大夫　嗎？
_____ Aren't you all doctors?

_____ Not all the teachers are nice.

_____ None of the cars are American cars.

_____ None of my friends are Chinese either.

2) NOTES ON GRAMMAR: A Chinese question word (QW), such as
谁，哪　　is not always　placed at the beginning of a question,
while its English counterpart (who,which) is always transposed to the beginning of a question.
DO NOT use a "嗎" in a QW question.
QW + ( 不) + V/SV + (O) ?
==========================

誰　不　好　　？
_____ Who is not nice?

_____ Who is your friend?

_____Who is not busy?

_____Whose car is big?

S + ( 不) + V + QW + (的) + N ?
==========================

這　　　　是　哪　　　國　車 ?
_____ Which country's car is this?
(Where is the car from?)

_____ Whose teacher is she?

_____ Who are you?

_____ Whose doctor is she?

_____ Which country (Where) are you from?

_____ Which country is that?

3) NOTES ON GRAMMAR: An adjective is used to modify the noun which follows it,
Ex: 好媽媽 (good mother). Note that a 的 must be used after the adjective in the following
cases.
 a) When the adjective is modified by an adverb,　　Ex: 很好的媽媽
 b) When the adjective is more than one syllable, Ex:好看(good looking)的車
很 + Adj + 的 + N
=====================

很　大　的　車
_____very big car

_____very nice doctor

_____very busy friend

_____very big country

## 12. CROSSWORD PUZZLE:

Fill in the puzzle in Chinese characters:

CLUES

Horizontal: 1) Both your father and mother are nice.

2) This is the doctor's.

3) That is an old car.

5) Where are you from?

10) Is a nice car big?　　11) Who is busy?

Vertical:　1) Are you a teacher?

2) This is my friend.

3) Who is that?

4) Is it?

5) You are all Americans.

6) Are all big cars good?

7) Good teachers are all very busy.

8) Is mother's car very big?

9) Are all books good?

12) good car

Fill in the puzzle in PINYIN:

## CLUES

Horizontal:
1) Whose car
2) good person
3) which country
4) China
5) mother
6) they
7) I am busy.
8) elder brother
9) Chinese language
14) book
15) good one
16) all

Vertical:
10) me
11) She is not busy.
12) old person
13) busy

Write down the phrase which goes diagonally 1):

_____ (Speak Chinese.)

# LESSONS 7,8,9

1.  Circle the right tone:

| | | | | | | | | | |
|---|---|---|---|---|---|---|---|---|---|
| 1) | jiāo | ji ǎo | jiāo | jiáo | 11) | guí | guì | guǐ | guī |
| 2) | xǐng | xìng | xíng | xīng | 12) | kē | ké | kě | kè |
| 3) | cháng | chāng | chàng | chǎng | 13) | shéng | shěng | shèng | shēng |
| 4) | wǎi | wài | wāi | wái | 14) | wéi | wěi | wēi | wèi |
| 5) | jǐng | jíng | jǐng | jìng | 15) | jīn | jín | jǐn | jìn |
| 6) | huàn | huán | huān | huǎn | 16) | qíng | qǐng | qìng | qīng |
| 7) | yuān | yuàn | yuán | yuǎn | 17) | xī | xí | xì | xǐ |
| 8) | shēn | shèn | shēn | shén | 18) | jiǎng | jiāng | jiáng | jiàng |
| 9) | qī | qí | qǐ | qì | 19) | huáng | huāng | huǎng | huàng |
| 10) | liú | liù | liū | liǔ | 20) | yǎn | yàn | yān | yàn |

2.  Add the correct tone marks to the following disyllabic words:

| | | | | | |
|---|---|---|---|---|---|
| 1) | niunai | 11) | keqi | 21) | Shanghai |
| 2) | shenme | 12) | shijie | 22) | Faguo |
| 3) | Meiguo | 13) | pijiu | 23) | hanyu |
| 4) | Dayang Zhou | 14) | na guo ren | 24) | huang he |
| 5) | women | 15) | laoshi | 25) | daifu |
| 6) | ditu | 16) | xiansheng | 26) | xiexie |
| 7) | xi yan | 17) | chang jiang | 27) | shenme ditu |
| 8) | Deguo | 18) | Riben che | 28) | Nan Meı Zhou |
| 9) | Chang cheng | 19) | taiṭai | 29) | taiyang |
| 10) | qing jin | 20) | he cha | 30) | Zhongguo |

3.  Choose the correct one:

| | | | | | | | | | |
|---|---|---|---|---|---|---|---|---|---|
| 1) | xī | jī | qī | 4) | xié | jié | 7) | yuē | yū |
| 2) | jiǎn | qiǎn | | 5) | rǎo | shǎo | 8) | yuán | yán |
| 3) | qìng | xìng | | 6) | jìn | qìng | 9) | zhīdào | chídào |

4.  Dictation in Pinyin with tone marks:

| | | |
|---|---|---|
| 1) | 6) | |
| 2) | 7) | |
| 3) | 8) | |
| 4) | 9) | |
| 5) | 10) | |

5. Listen and choose the correct response.

1)   a.   b.

2)   a.   b.

3)   a.   b.

4)   a.   b.

5)   a.   b.

6)   a.   b.

6. Listen and fill in the blanks.

1) 我們 ＿＿＿ 不 ＿＿＿＿＿ 。　你＿＿＿?

2) 請 ＿＿＿ ，請＿＿＿＿ 。　謝謝，不 ＿＿＿＿ 。

3) 那是 ＿＿＿ 國＿＿＿＿ ?

4) 你＿＿＿＿ ?　你是 ＿＿＿＿＿＿＿ 嗎 ?

7. Listen to each dialogue and check the statements as right(V) or wrong(X).

1) (   ) 他們都吸美國煙。
   (   ) 美國煙很好，也很貴。

2) (   ) 他們都是留學生。
   (   ) 他們都吸煙。

3) (   ) 中國茶好喝。
   (   ) 他們不都喝茶。

4) (   ) B　看中國地圖。

5) (　) Wang Yun　請　Mr.Li 喝茶。

　　(　) Mr.Li 叫Dazhong。

6) (　) Palanka　爸爸媽媽看Wang老師。

　　(　) Wang 老師歡迎他們。

8. Practice the following characters.

| | | |
|---|---|---|
| 什 | 客 | 外 |
| 麼 | 氣 | 院 |
| 地 | 吸 | 習 |
| 圖 | 煙 | 貴 |
| 看 | 謝 | 姓 |
| 請 | 問 | 叫 |
| 進 | 留 | 您 |
| 歡 | 學 | 喝 |
| 迎 | 生 | 茶 |

Find the characters which share the same initial stroke as the ones shown below.

Please also include　characters from the previous lessons.

Note: A stroke may vary in length.

客:

什:

圖:

9. Fill in the blanks with 誰、誰的、的、貴、叫、都、什麼、哪國、姓、貴：

1) 您＿＿＿姓？我＿＿＿丁，＿＿＿中生。

2) 這是 ＿＿＿＿＿＿ 漢語書？ 是我 ＿＿＿ 。

3) ＿＿＿ 學漢語？ 我們＿＿＿ 學。

4) 你喝 ＿＿＿＿＿ 茶？

5) ＿＿＿＿＿＿車好，也不 ＿＿＿？

10. GUIDED COMPOSITION (Word order & sentence order):
    Rearrange the words in each entry to make a grammatical sentence.
Rearrange the sentences in the correct order to make a meaningful passage.

1) 學習　嗎　漢語　你

2) 哪國　是　你　留學生　請問

3) 留學生　中國　是　我，　呢　你

4) 是　法國　我　留學生

5) 漢語　不　學　我

6) 學習　漢語　我　朋友　古波

7) 很　的　好　漢語　他

The correct sentence order: ＿＿2＿＿＿＿＿＿＿＿＿＿＿＿＿．

11. TRANSLATION: Translate the following sentences into Chinese, using the illustrated patterns.
NOTES ON GRAMMAR: The structure of a simple SVO(subject+verb+object) sentence is
the same as is in English.

S + ( 不 ) + V + O + ( 嗎 )
==========================

老師　　看　中文書。_____ The teacher reads Chinese books.

(Zhōngwén:Chinese language)

_____ She doesn't smoke American cigarettes.

_____ Do you drink Chinese tea?

Imperative sentences:
( 請 ) + V + O
===============

請　喝　茶! _____ Please have some tea.

_____ Please look at the map.

_____ Please study Chinese.

NOTES ON GRAMMAR: QW 什麼, like the other QWs, is not always placed at the beginning of a question. (See page 19 (2).)

什麼 + S + ( 不 ) SV　?
========================

什麼 茶　　好喝　? _____ What tea is good to drink ?

_____ What (kind of ) car is not expensive?

S + ( 不 ) + V + 什麼 + (O)　?
============================

你　喝　什麼　? _____ What do you drink?

_____ What does he study?

_____ What cigarette do you not smoke?

## 12. CROSSWORD PUZZLE:

CLUES

Horizontal:

1) foreigner

2) Old people also drink.

3) All are fine.

4) All teachers are good.

5) to study what?

6) All teas are good.

7) What doesn't the teacher drink?

8) What is your (honorable)surname?

9) Have a cigarette please!

11) May I ask...?

12) welcome him

15) Have (drink) some tea!

Vertical:

1) Foreign Language Institute

2) All teachers drink tea.

4) old friend

7) The teacher asks.

8) What do you drink?

10) Cigarettes are all expensive.

11) Please come in!

13) You ask him.

14) They also drink.

**13. Translate the following dialogue into both Pinyin(in bubbles) and characters:**

A:Excuse me(May I ask), are you Doctor Xie ( 謝 )?

B: Yes, I am. What is your name?

A: I am Alice Smith.

B: Alice, how are you? Please come in!

A: Thank you.

B: Please sit down.

A: Thank you.

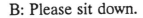

B: Alice, where are you from?

A: I am a foreign student from Canada.( 加拿大 Jiānádà)

B: What are you studying?

A: I am studying Chinese. Your father is my teacher.

B: I am Alice's mother.

A: Mrs. Smith, how are you? Welcome!

Smith 太太.

B: Thank you.

B: Do you smoke?

A: I don't smoke. Thank you.

B: Do you drink Chinese tea?

A: Yes, I do.

B: Please have some tea!

A: Thank you for your tea.

B: You are welcome. Good bye! (再见)

A: Good bye!

# LESSONS 10,11,12

1. Choose the correct one:

   1) zī          cī                    7) haízi        shéngzi
   2) zuò         cuò                   8) zuò cāo      zuò cuò
   3) zǎo         cǎo                   9) xǐ zǎo       bá cǎo
   4) zài         cài                  10) xiànzài      gāngcái
   5) zéng        céng                 11) zēngzǐ       céngcì
   6) zùn         cùn                  12) zǔnshǒu      cūnzi

2. Dictation in Pinyin with tone marks:

   1)              6)              11)
   2)              7)              12)
   3)              8)              13)
   4)              9)              14)
   5)             10)              15)

3. Listen and choose the correct translation:

   1) Where does he come from?            a  b  c
   2) What is your full name?             a  b  c
   3) Where do you live?                  a  b  c
   4) How mang students study Chinese?    a  b  c
   5) Whom do you often visit   ?         a  b  c

4. Listening comprehension:  Listen to the dialogue twice and mark the
   following as right or wrong:

   1) Dialogue one:

   (  )  The conversation is  between a mother and her daughter.
   (  )  The daughter is going to visit  her mother.
   (  )  The daughter's friend is living in the dormitory.
   (  )  The Chinese student wants to borrow their car.
   (  )  The daughter is studying English literature.

   2) Dialogue two:

   (  )  The conversation took place in a dormitory.
   (  )  Mali lives in Room 40, 10th floor.
   (  )  The telephone number of the dormitory is 96-1378.
   (  )  The conversation is between Mali and her friend.

5. Practice the following characters:

| | | | |
|---|---|---|---|
| 坐 | 詞 | 一 | |
| 住 | 典 | 二 | |
| 宿 | 畫 | 三 | |
| 多 | 報 | 四 | |
| 舍 | 五 | 再 | |
| 號 | 見 | 六 | |
| 在 | 還 | 七 | |
| 少 | 先 | 八 | |
| 層 | 英 | 九 | |
| 兒 | 認 | 十 | |
| 現 | 識 | 下 | |
| 用 | 法 | 女 | |
| 去 | 她 | 常 | |

Find the characters which share the same initial stroke as the ones given below.
Please also include characters from the previous lessons.
Note that a stroke may vary in length.

兒:

現:

詞:

常:

6. Find the correct response and write the letter in the parenthesis:

( )1.還你词典，謝謝。　　　　　A.五層十三號。
( )2.你的宿舍在多少層?多少號?　B.我也不認識他。
( )3.你去哪兒?　　　　　　　　C.不是，是我哥哥的。
( )4.他叫什麼名字?　　　　　　D.謝謝，我不吸。
( )5.你常去哪兒?　　　　　　　E.常去大學。
( )6.他是你的女朋友嗎?　　　　F.我弟弟的法語老師。
( )7.這是誰的畫報?　　　　　　G.六十八號。
( )8.你的弟弟住多少號?　　　　H.去看老師。
( )9.請吸煙!　　　　　　　　　I.是老師的。
( )10. 他是誰?　　　　　　　　J.不客氣。

7. GUIDED COMPOSITION (Word order & Sentence order):

Rearrange the words in each entry to make a grammatical sentence.
Rearrange the sentences in the correct order to make a meaningful passage. Choose an appropriate topic for the passage.

A) 住　學生宿舍　九層　她　十三號

B) 茶　常　我們　去　喝

C) 是　留學生　美云　中國

D) 叫　女　謝大夫　朋友　的　美云

E) 朋友　他們　是　都　好　我的

F) 她　去　宿舍　謝大夫　看　常

The correct sentence order: D_____.

An appropriate topic : _____.

-33-

8. Fill in the blanks:

1) ＿＿＿ 問，謝老師在嗎？他＿＿＿＿＿.
2) 你朋友還你 ＿＿＿＿＿＿＿＿ ？ 還我書。
3) ＿＿＿ 進，＿＿＿坐，＿＿＿喝＿＿＿。
4) "謝謝！" "不＿＿＿＿＿！"
5) ＿＿＿ 在他不學＿＿＿語，學＿＿＿語。
6) 他住＿＿＿＿＿＿層＿＿＿＿＿＿號？
7) 用 ＿＿＿＿＿＿＿＿ 你的車，好＿＿＿？
8) 請＿＿＿，您貴姓？ 我＿＿＿謝。
9) 你常去＿＿＿＿＿＿看書？
10) 那不是中國地圖，是＿＿＿＿＿＿地圖？
11) 那是＿＿＿的車？是哥哥的。
12) 這是 ＿＿＿＿＿＿ 書？是漢語書。

## 9.TRANSLATION:

Translate the following sentences into Chinese, using the illustrated patterns.

1) NOTES ON GRAMMAR: A time word(TW) such as 現在 (now), 一號(1st day of a month),etc. is placed either before or after the subject，but never at the end of a sentence.

(TW) +S + (TW)+ Adv + V/SV +(O)+ ( 嗎)
========================

現在 你 忙 嗎 ? _____Are you busy now?

_____I am going to China on the 11th.

_____His father is not using his car now.

_____I am not using the dictionary now.

_____Does he often come to the dormitory now?

_____Where are you now?

_____I'll return the book on the 10th.

(2) NOTES ON GRAMMAR: The QW 多少(how many, how much), like other QWs, is not necessarily placed at the beginning of a question.(See P.19 & 27.)

多少 ＋ S ＋ V ＋(O) ?
=====================

多少　學生　學習　漢語？＿＿＿＿ How many students study Chinese?

＿＿＿＿＿＿＿＿＿＿＿＿＿＿＿＿＿ How many people drink tea?

＿＿＿＿＿＿＿＿＿＿＿＿＿＿＿＿＿ How many people live in the dormitory?

＿＿＿＿＿＿＿＿＿＿＿＿＿＿＿＿＿ How many students use a Chinese dictionary?

S ＋ V ＋ 多少 ＋O ?
=====================

你　　認識　多少　　漢字？＿＿ How many characters do you know?

＿＿＿＿＿＿＿＿＿＿＿＿＿＿＿＿＿ How many foreign languages do you study?

＿＿＿＿＿＿＿＿＿＿＿＿＿＿＿＿＿ How many dictionaries do you use?

(3) NOTES ON GRAMMAR: 多 (many, much) and 少(few, little) are also adjectives, but they can not be used to modify a noun without an adverb, such as 很.

Note that 的 is optional after 多 and 少.

书多　　画报少

很多 / 很少+(的) S + (Adv)+ V/SV +(O)
==========================

很多　　　學生　　　學習漢語。Many students study Chinese.

＿＿＿＿＿＿＿＿＿＿＿＿＿＿＿＿＿ Few people don't smoke nowadays.

＿＿＿＿＿＿＿＿＿＿＿＿＿＿＿＿＿ Few books and pictorials are good.

＿＿＿＿＿＿＿＿＿＿＿＿＿＿＿＿＿ Many friends are going to China.

(4) NOTES ON GRAMMAR: In a sentence with more than one verb phrase, the first verb phrase usually has a 來 or 去 to indicate coming or going somewhere to do something.

S + (Adv.) 來 / 去 + place + V + (O)

======================

（dàxué）

我　　　去　　大學　學習。 _____I go to university to study.

_____He doesn't often　go to visit his father.

_____She often goes to the dormitory to see friends.

_____He is going to the university to thank her.

_____Where are we going to welcome the foreign students?

10. Change the following sentences into questions by using the QWs - 哪，哪兒，什麼，多少，誰. Make as many questions as possible.

1) 哥哥常去醫院 (yīyuàn-hospital) 看大夫。

　　Ex:
　　　　誰常去醫院看大夫？
　　　　哥哥常去哪兒看大夫？
　　　　哥哥常去醫院看誰？

2) 很多人在大學 (dàxué:university）學習漢語。

3) 爸爸的美國車很貴.

-36-

## 11. CROSSWORD PUZZLE:

CLUES:

Horizontal:
1) What number is your room?
   (Which room do you live?)
2) She returns the pictorial.
3) Study what?
4) study Chinese
5) Who lives in No. 40?
6) He doesn't know me either.
8) What do you use?
9) She is pretty.(好看)
12) The dictionary is expensive.
14) Go to the 10th floor.

Vertical:
1) Where are you going to study?
2) What book does he use?
3) study French
5) Who lives on the 14th floor?
6) Which floor does he live?
7) No. 4
9) What dictionary does she return?
10) I don't read newspaper.(報)
11) Is a car expensive?
13) I don't know Chinese characters.

## 12. GUIDED DIALOGUE:

Rearrange the words to make a meaningful dialogue.

A: 喂！ Alice，好久不見了！ (Long time no see) 你好嗎？
（ Hǎo jiǔ bú jiàn le ）

B:_____( 很好。好嗎都爸爸媽媽？ )

A:_____( 都他們好很，也忙很都)

A:_____(什麼你看 )

B:_____( 是　這　法語　畫報 )

A:_____ (畫報　看　常　也　我)

_____(畫報　多　很　我的 )

_____( 看　你　歡迎)

B:_____ (謝謝，看　不　你　嗎? )

A:_____ (看　現在　我　不。)

B:_____ (多謝，一號　還　你　我)
(1st day of a month)

A:_____ (客氣　不。)

B:_____ ( 你不忙，來　坐一下兒
我們　宿舍　請)

A:_____ ( 好，看你　宿舍去　我)

A & B: 再見!

-38-

# LESSON 13

1. Listen to each question and circle the correct answer:

1) a. 去商店　　b. 買紙　　　　c. 看書
2) a. 不學中文　b. 學英文　　　c. 是的
3) a. 美國留學生　b. 加拿大人好　　c. 那國學生
4) a. 在哪兒　　b. 不在　　　　c. 加拿大(Canada)
5) a. 我介紹　　b. 認識　　　　c. 在哪兒

Notes:
中文zhōngwén：漢語
　美國Měiguó：America
　加拿大Jiānádà：Canada
　英文yīngwén：英語

2. Listen to each sentence and write in Pinyin. Pay attention to the change of tone of "不".

1)　　　　　　　　　　6)

2)　　　　　　　　　　7)

3)　　　　　　　　　　8)

4)　　　　　　　　　　9)

5)　　　　　　　　　　10)

3. Listen and write in characters. Translate them into English.

1)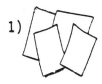

四张纸
(four pieces of paper)

3)

2)

来(來)

4. Listen and write the following classroom expressions in Pinyin:

1) Do the exercise.

2) Please look at the book.

3) Please listen again.

4) Please say it again.

5) Do you understand?

6) Is it correct?

7) Please answer.

8) Do you have any questions?

9) Please say it in Chinese.

10) Class is over, good-bye!

教室

4. Practice the following characters.

| 字 | 介 | 名 |
|---|---|---|
| 紹 | 喂 | 男 |
| 啊 | 對 | 商 |
| 和 | 店 | 說 |
| 買 | 筆 | 來 |

6.TRANSLATION: Translate the following sentences into Chinese, using the illustrated patterns:

(1) NOTES ON GRAMMAR: Note that a "的" must be used between a noun and its modifier when the modifier is more than one syllable. (See p.20.)

(Mod. 的 )S + (Adv.) + SV/V + (Mod. 的) + (O)

========================================

不貴的 車 不 多 _____ Inexpensive cars are not many.

_____ I often go to the big stores.

_____ We are good friends.

_____ Many beautiful paintings are very expensive.
　　　　　　　　　　　( 好看 )( 畫兒)

_____ Busy people don't go to stores often.


(2)NOTES ON GRAMMAR: "和(and)" is used to join nouns or pronouns, not sentences. Note that one can not say "我去和他也去。"

S1 ( 和 S2) + (Adv) + V/SV + (O1 和 O2)

==============================

我　　　　　　　　買 本子和詞典. I buy books and dictionaries.

_____ Japanese and Chinese all drink tea.

_____ Pen and paper are all inexpensive.


(3) NOTES ON GRAMMAR: "都" qualifies only the words preceding it, therefore it is necessary to transpose the object which is qualified by 都 to the beginning of the sentence or after the subject.


Ex: I love both my parents.
Wrong- 我愛都媽媽和爸爸。 or 我都愛爸爸和媽媽。
Right- 爸爸和媽媽我都愛。 or 我爸爸媽媽都愛。

O + S +（ 不 ）都（ 不) + V

========================

筆和紙　我　　都　　　買。　　　I buy both pen and paper.

_____We welcome both teachers and students.

_____I use neither a book nor a dictionary.

_____ He doesn't read all the Chinese newspapers.

(4) NOTES ON GRAMMAR: In an Affirmative-negative question, the object can be placed after either verb.

Ex:　你買筆不買？　or　你買不買筆？

S + V (O) + 不 + V (O)　?

========================

你　　吸煙　　不　　吸 ?　_____ Do you smoke or not?

_____ Do you speak Chinese or not?

_____ Does he buy a car or not?

(5) When an affirmative-negative question has more than one verb, the negative particle "不" goes with the first verb or the adverb "常".

S + V1 + 不 + V1 + V2 + O ?

========================

你　　來　不　來　　學　漢語?____Are you coming to study Chinese ?

_____ Are you going to visit your friends ?

_____ Does he go to drink tea ?

S ＋ 常 ＋ 不 ＋ 常 ＋ V ＋ O ?
====================

他 常 不 常 用詞典？ Does he often use a dictionary ?
_____ Does he often speak Chinese or not?

_____ Do you come here often or not?

_____ Does your mother go to see a doctor oftcn or not?

7. Make sentences by matching words from part I to those from part II. Draw a line to connect them.

1) 我去書店　　　　　　　　　　多少號？
2) 他來郵局 (yóujú:post office)　　教什麼課？
3) 帕蘭卡的爸爸在大學　　　　　買筆和紙。
4) 你去哪兒　　　　　　　　　　誰的書？
5) 請問這是　　　　　　　　　　是哪國人？
6) 你去商店　　　　　　　　　　介紹一下兒。
7) 歡迎！請進！我給你們　　　　看朋友？
8) 你哥哥認識　　　　　　　　　買什麼？
9) 你朋友住　　　　　　　　　　買郵票。(yóupiào:stamp)
10) 你的漢語老師　　　　　　　　不認識我的大夫？

8. Reading comprehension: Read the text on page 132, and check the following statements as right(V) or wrong(X).

( )1. 帕蘭卡和古波都認識丁云。
( )2. 古波和丁云都學習漢語。
( )3. 丁云介紹帕蘭卡和古波認識。
( )4. 古波問丁云學什麼？
( )5. 丁云的爸爸和媽媽也都很忙。
( )6. 王 (Wang) 老師常去宿舍看古波和帕蘭卡。
( )7. 古波學英語和法語。
( )8. 帕蘭卡，丁云，古波不都是學生。
( )9. 帕蘭卡，丁云，古波都不是中國人。
( )10. 古波不説漢語.

9. Find the traditional character and write it beside its simplified form:

纸 (　) 詞　　　谁 (　) 謝　　　学 (　) 兒
绍 (　) 識　　　请 (　) 誰　　　习 (　) 號
认 (　) 紙　　　谢 (　) 門　　　儿 (　) 氣
识 (　) 認　　　贵 (　) 請　　　号 (　) 習
词 (　) 紹　　　门 (　) 貴　　　气 (　) 學

10. MIND-STRETCHERS:.

這個宿舍很大，很多留學生住在這兒。
四十六個學生會 (huì:know how to) 説法語；三十九個學生會説英語。
這些 (zhèxiē:these) 學生，二十四個會説英語，也會説法語。

Questions: Answer the following questions and also explain your reasoning.
Suggested vocabulary:　因爲(yīnwèi:because)
　　　　　　　　　所以(suǒyǐ:therefore)

(1)　這個宿舍住多少留學生？

(2)　多少學生只 (zhǐ:only) 會説法語？

(3)　多少學生只會説英語？

宿舍

Notes:　個(ge) is a measure word(MW). See Lesson 15 for its usage.

## 11. SEEK AND FIND:

From the following jumble of characters, find as many sentences or Verb-object phrases as possible. Look horizontally, vertically and diagonally. Circle them. (There are 17 altogether.)

| | | | | | | | | |
|---|---|---|---|---|---|---|---|---|
| 他 | 來 | 宿 | 舍 | 誰 | 請 | 喝 | 茶 | 介 | 紹 |
| 她 | 看 | 去 | 商 | 店 | 買 | 筆 | 誰 | 看 | 我 |
| 你 | 的 | 書 | 和 | 畫 | 報 | 都 | 是 | 我 | 的 |
| 去 | 茶 | 店 | 介 | 喂 | 和 | 不 | 王 | 和 | 媽 |
| 那 | 兒 | 買 | 啊 | 紹 | 給 | 貴 | 先 | 我 | 媽 |
| 二 | 什 | 書 | 多 | 少 | 男 | 學 | 生 | 哥 | 不 |
| 麼 | 名 | 你 | 有 | 多 | 少 | 朋 | 友 | 哥 | 來 |
| 朋 | 友 | 的 | 中 | 國 | 名 | 字 | 友 | 說 | 會 |

---

BODY LANGUAGE: Guess what these Chinese body language mean. Circle a or b.

 Raise the right arm and move the right hand up and down.
a) Good bye.
b) Come here.

 Give something with both hand.
a) to show respect
b) to ask if it is enough

 Pat the forehead with the right hand palm.
a) How stupid I am!
b) Now I got it!

 Scratch the head.
a) My head is itchy badly.
b) It's tough. I am thinking.

 Make a circle with the thumb and the index finger.
a) It's perfect.
b) It's a zero; nothing

## 12. GUIDED CONVERSATION:

Write a dialogue, using the suggested words.

Add more questions and answers to complete the dialogue.

### 1) Getting to know each other:

A: _____ （ 是　我John Smith,
姓　貴　您?)

B: _____ （ 叫　我　丁美，
好　你!)

B: _____ （ 是　你　人　國　哪?)

A: ___加拿大人，_____?

B: _____

### 2) Asking someone where he is going:

A: _____ （ 喂　哪兒　你　去
老謝?)

B: _____ （ 我　買　詞典书店。)
書店　去.)

A: _____

B: _____

### 3) Introducing people:

A: _____ （ 都　你們　認識　不,
一下兒　來　我
介紹.)

A: _____ (是　這....,是　這....)

B: _____

C: _____

A: _____

-46-

# LESSON 14

1. Listen to each sentence, then write in Pinyin and characters:

  1).

  2)

  3)

  4)

  5)

2. Listen to each sentence, then translate into English:

  1)

  2)

  3)

  4)

  5)

  6)

3. Listen and choose the correct response:

  1) a.     2) a.     3) a.     4) a.     5) a.     6) a.

     b.        b.        b.        b.        b.        b.

4. Listen to each dialogue and check the statements as right(V) or wrong(X):

Dialogue I: (　　) a. 妹妹沒有孩子。
　　　　　　(　　) b. 妹妹不工作。
Dialogue II:(　　) a. 男人和女人都去書店。
　　　　　　(　　) b. 女人在書店工作。

6. Listen and fill in the blanks.

1) 我家有 ＿＿＿＿＿ ＿＿＿＿＿ ＿＿＿＿＿ ＿＿＿＿＿ 和 ＿＿＿＿＿ 。

2) 我不 ＿＿＿＿＿ 你我＿＿＿＿＿誰 ＿＿＿＿＿ 。

3) 他 ＿＿＿＿＿ 不在 ＿＿＿＿＿ ＿＿＿＿＿ 。

4) 請 ＿＿＿＿＿ 你的家人 ＿＿＿＿＿ 。

5) 姐姐的＿＿＿＿＿都是 ＿＿＿＿＿ 。

6. Practice the following characters:

| 銀 | 行 | 工 |
|---|---|---|
| 作 | 想 | 家 |
| 沒 | 有 | 孩 |
| 子 | 告 | 訴 |
| 給 | 寫 | 信 |
| 姐 | 妹 | 愛 |

我給你書。

-48-

7. TRANSLATION: Translate the following sentences into Chinese, using the illustrated patterns:

1) NOTES ON GRAMMAR: Prepositonal phrases (PP) with 給 and 在

A prepositional phrase(prep.+ N) precedes the main verb in a sentence, while its English counterpart is always post-verbal.

S+ Adv(不 / 都 / 常 )+PP( 給 +N)+V+(O)+( 嗎 )
==================================

我　不　常　　　給爸爸媽媽寫信. I don't often write to my parents.

_____My friend is returning the book for me.

_____He is buying a car for his mother.

_____Please buy a Chinese book for me.

_____Do all of you write to your friends often?

S + Adv + PP( 在 +place)+V+(O)+ ( 嗎 )
==============================

你　　在哪兒　　買 茶?　　　Where do you buy tea?

_____He is not studying Chinese at home.

_____Does your sister work at the bank?

_____My father does not work at the university.

_____What do you buy at the bookstore?

-49-

2) NOTES ON GRAMMAR: Unlike the other verbs, the negative form of 有 is 沒有，never 不有 . Verb 有 in Chinese may incdicate either possession (to have) or existence (there is/there are).

S + Adv + 有 / 沒有 + O + ( 嗎 ) ?
========================

沒有，我們都沒有.     你們有沒有漢語詞典?

學生 都 有 詞典 嗎?    Do all students have dictionaries?

_____ Doctor Ding( 丁 ) does not have children.

_____ Neither one of us has a car.

_____ There are no foreign students in our university.

The affirmative-negative question, using 有:

S + Adv.+ 有沒有 + O ?
========================

書店 有沒有 漢語詞典? Are there any Chinese dictionaries in the bookstore?

_____Do you all have brothers and sisters?

_____Are there any female clerks( 職員 )in the bank?

_____Do you have a boy friend?

_____Is there any one at the bank?

_____Do you have any cigarettes?

我不吸烟.

-50-

8. Fill in the blanks with　有、是、不是、不、給、沒有、在：

1) 你有 _____ 中國地圖？我 _____ 很多。

2) 他 _____ 哪兒工作？　他 _____ 書店工作。

3) 你姐姐是工程師 _____？ _____ ，他是工程師。

4) 請問你 _____ 大學學習嗎？你忙 ____ 忙？

5) 請他 _____ 我們介紹一下兒那個銀行。

6) 我常 _____ 媽媽寫信，不常 _____ 妹妹寫信。

7) 你哥哥 _____ 學生，你弟弟也 ____ 學生嗎？

9. READING COMPREHENSION:
Read the text on page 153 and answer the following questions:
1) 哥哥弟弟姐姐妹妹，帕蘭卡都有嗎？

2) 保爾是誰？

3) 帕蘭卡的爸爸和媽媽作什麼工作？

4) 帕蘭卡會 (huì:know) 不會法語？

5) 帕蘭卡的家，誰學習？

## 10. MIND-STRETCHERS:

### 誰作什麼工作？ WHO IS DOING WHAT?

Wang

老王、老丁和老謝三個人在一個商店工作。這個商店有三個工作:
工人，職員和經理。職員的工錢最少，他的爸爸媽媽只有一個孩子。
老王的愛人是老丁的妹妹。老王的工錢最多，他也不是經理。
請問，他們三個人，誰作什麼工作？

Vacabulary:

| | | |
|---|---|---|
| 工人 | gōngrén | worker |
| 工錢 | gōngqián | wage |
| 最少 | zuì shǎo | least |
| 最多 | zuì duō | most |
| 只 | zhǐ | only |

老王　老丁　老謝

工人　職員　經理

Please write the process of your reasoning in Chinese.

Ex: 因為 (yīnwèi:because) 老王的工錢最多，職員的工錢最少，
所以 (suǒyǐ:therefore) 老王不是職員。

# LESSON 15

1. Listen and write the numerals:

   1)          2)          3)          4)

   5)          6)          7)          8)

   9)        10)        11)        12)

   13)       14)       15)       16)

2. Listen, and answer the following questions in Pinyin and characters.

   1)

   2)

   3)

   4)

   5) huì:can

   6) (běr=běn)

   7) (něige=nǎge)

   8)

3. LISTENING COMPREHENSION: Listen to the dialogue and mark the following as right(✔) or wrong ( X ).
   1) (　) Ding Yun jiā yǒu wǔge rén.
   2) (　) Ding Yun yǒu yíge gēge hé yíge mèimei.
   3) (　) Ding Yun de gēge zài yóujú mài yóupiào.

4) (    ) Ding Yun de bàba zài yínháng gōngzuò.

5) (    ) Ding Yun de māma zài yóujú gōngzuò.

6) (    ) Ding Yun jiā de rén dōu gōngzuò.

4. Listen and choose the correct response:

1) a     2) a     3) a     4) a     5) a

     b        b        b        b        b

5. Listen and fill in the blanks:

1) 你們中文 ＿＿＿ 有 ＿＿＿＿＿＿＿ 老師？有＿＿＿＿＿＿＿。

2) ＿＿＿＿＿＿＿ 室有很＿＿＿哪國雜＿＿＿和畫＿＿＿？

3) 誰＿＿＿你們＿＿＿語？ 誰＿＿＿你們＿＿＿漢字？

4) ＿＿＿ 的中文很＿＿＿。 不敢＿＿＿。我們＿＿＿＿＿＿＿學習。

6. Practice the following characters:

| 教 | 口 | 敢 |
|---|---|---|
| 當 | 互 | 相 |
| 新 | 閱 | 覽 |
| 室 | 中 | 文 |
| 系 | 個 | 幾 |
| 雜 | 誌 | 本 |
| 館 | | |

7. TRANSLATION:Translate the following sentences into Chinese, using the illustrated patterns.

(1) NOTES ON GRAMMAR: In modern Chinese, a Measure Word (MW) must be attached to the following words - 這 , 那 , 哪 , 幾 or a numeral (1,2,3....), when they are followed by a noun(or a noun phrase).

Note that before some nouns, such as 國 (country), 班 (class), 天 (day), 年(year),etc., no MW is needed. 多少 does not require a MW either.

Use "這 / 那 / 哪 / 幾 /1,2..+ MW+N " in your translation.

你有幾本中文書? _____How many Chinese books do you have?

_____That magazine is mine.

_____How many teachers are there in this department?

_____In China, one family has    one child.

_____Which department has two reading rooms?

_____How many characters do you know now?

Note: In some cases, the function of a MW is similar to "one" in English.

Ex: 哪個是你的? _____Which one is yours?

_____This one is pretty.

_____I'll buy 20 (of something).

_____That one is very expensive.

_____Which one would you like to have?

-55-

(2) NOTES ON GRAMMAR: Adverbs 還 (hái:furthermore, in addition) and 也(also):
Adverbs 還 and 也 are placed before a verb, a stative verb or another adverb.
還 and 也 are different in usage from 和 and can not be used to join nouns.(See lesson 13.)
Ex: Wrong-　我買書也報。　or　我買書還報。
　　Right-　我買書也買報。　or　我買書，還買報。
　　　or　　我買書和報。

Sentence 1 , S +　也 / 還 +(PP) + V + (O)
============================

他學習，他　還　在銀行　工作。 He studies, furthermore he also works at the bank.

_____ He knows me, he also knows my friend.

_____ I am buying a dictionary and also three books.

_____ I love my elder sister and also my younger sister.

_____ She has an elder brother, and also a younger brother.

(3) NOTES ON GRAMMAR: Adverb 互相 is used only with a limited number of verbs.
Ex:　互相學習 (learn from each other) and 互相幫助(help each other)。

S + (　常　) +　互相 + V
==================

我朋友和我　常　互相　學習。 My friend and I often learn from each other.

_____ Do doctors often learn from one another?

_____ Do you and your friend help each other?

-56-

8. GUIDED COMPOSITION (Word order & Sentence order):

Rearrange the words in each entry to make a grammatical sentence.

Rearrange the sentences to make a meaningful passage.

Give an appropriate topic for the passage.

A) 去 中國 想 很 她 看 我

B) 互相 寫信 我們 用 中文 常常

C) 名字 她 的 愛妹 叫

D) 工作 一家 現在 公司 愛妹 在

E) 有 我 女 一個 朋友 中國

F) 不 好 很 的 英語 她　　還

The correct sentence order: E_____

An appropriate topic:_____

9. Fill in blanks with 很 有 還 也 多少 和 几 給 給
1) 你們大學____多少學生____老師？
2) 他教我們語法，____教我們口語。
3) 圖書館有_____ 詞典？
4) 他家有____個人？
5) ____多學生學習中文嗎？
6) 他不借____ 我他的車。
7) 你常____ 誰寫信？
8) 我朋友還不____我書。

## 10. CROSSWORD PUZZLE:

Fill out the puzzle in Pinyin, and also write the words in characters.

When completed correctly, a WONDER WORD between the two bold lines will form.

PINYIN                                    CHARACTER

(            )

(            )

(            )

(            )

(            )

(            )

THE WONDER WORD: _____

Clues:

1) 學生都常去那兒看書，還書和借書。 2) 他教你。

3) 中國人都用這種 (zhǒng:kind) 字。 4) 這個國的人都説漢語。

5) 你在這兒看雜誌，畫報和報。 6) 這本書告訴你生词的意思 (yìsi:meaning) 。

大学生       中学生       小学生

## 11. MIND-STRETCHERS:

　　一個大學有一個中日文系。這個系不很大。只 (zhǐ:only) 有一個中文班
和一個日文班。中文班有九個學生；日文班有十二個學生。這二十一個學生，
有五個學中文，也學日文。
請問，這個中日文系一共 (yígòng:altogether) 有多少學生？

Logical reasoning:

日文班　中文班

幾個學生只學中文？　　　　　　四個 (9-5=4)
幾個學生只學日文？　　　　　　七個 (12-5=7)
幾個學生學日文，也學中文？　　五個

這個中日文系一共有十六個學生。 (4+7+5=16)

Do the following question ，　using the example given.
有很多老師去一個書店買词典。書店一共賣了(màile:sold)
十一本词典。兩個老師只買英漢词典；五個老師只買漢英词典。
請問，幾個老師買漢英，也買英漢词典？

## 13. GUIDED CONVERSATION:

1) Start the conversation by arranging the illustrations in order and number them;

2) Write at least 2 more questions and answers to finish the conversation.

Notes: 會 hui: know how to; can

Pay attention to the difference of 中國，中國人 and 中文：

| | |
|---|---|
| 中國 | China; Chinese (not people) |
| 中國人 | Chinese (people) |
| 中文 | Chinese (language) |
| 中文書 | Chinese book |
| 中文地圖 | Chinese map (map in Chinese) |
| 中國地圖 | map of China |
| 中國車 | Chinese car |
| 中國大夫 | Chinese doctor |

中国人多

# LESSON 16

1. Listen to each question and circle the correct answer:

1) a.　b.　c.

2) a.　b.　c.

3) a.　b.　c.

4) a.　b.　c.

5) a.　b.　c.

2) Listen and translate into English:

1)



2)



3)



4)



5)

3. LISTENING COMPREHENSION: Listen to each dialogue twice and circle the correct one:

(A)

1) A was looking for her (pants; jacket; shirt).

2) The color of her garment is (green; blue; red; black).

3) Her garment is (old; new).

4) A (found; did not find) her garment.

(B)

1) A is looking for a (manager; professor; engineer).

2) Zhang is working in a(company; bank; school) now.

3) A (found; did not find Zhang).

4. Listen and fill in the blanks:

1) 張＿＿＿給我們＿＿張＿＿＿， ＿＿ 我們 ＿＿ ＿＿ 劇。

2) 你＿＿什麼？ 我＿＿我的＿＿＿ ＿＿＿。

3) 我＿＿買一 ＿＿襯＿＿ 和一 ＿＿ ＿＿＿ 。

4) ＿＿＿ 你＿＿＿什麼 ＿＿＿ 去＿＿朋＿＿？ 那件＿＿的。

5) 你們＿＿他 ＿＿＿＿ 來我 ＿＿＿ ，好嗎？

6) 他＿＿從 ＿＿＿ 去 ＿＿＿＿ 還書。

7) 那＿＿書店不＿＿大。 ＿＿＿ 中文 ＿＿＿ 。

5. Listen and answer the following questions in Pinyin: (Give short answers.)

1)

2)

3)

4)

5)

6)

7)

8)

9)

10)

6. Practice the following characters:

| | | |
|---|---|---|
| 張 | 裙 | 太 |
| 票 | 兩 | 從 |
| 京 | 襯 | 找 |
| 劇 | 衫 | 舊 |
| 晚 | 綠 | 穿 |
| 上 | 白 | 件 |
| 條 | | |

7. TRANSLATION: Translate the following sentences into Chinese, using the illustrated patterns.

1) NOTES ON GRAMMAR: The following "是....的" pattern is used to describe the ownership or condition of the subject.

Note the structural difference between (A) and (B).

A) 這本書很新。　(This book is very new.)

B) 這本書是新的。　(This book is a new one.)

but not: 這本書是新。

S　+　Adv　+　是　+　SV/Pro./N　+　的　+(嗎)

====================

他的襯衫都是　新　　　的　嗎? _____ Are all his shirts new(ones)?

_____ Whose dictionary is this?

_____ This car is my father's.

_____ Not all my skirts are green.

_____ Is this ticket yours?

2) NOTES ON GRAMMAR:

The prepositional phrase "從 + place" is usually followed by 來 or 去 and it functions like other prepositional phrases. (See P.49 在 and 給)

S+PP( 從 +place)+ 來 / 去 + place+(V)+(O)
=======================

他　從他家　　　　去　大學　學習。He is going to the college to study from his house.

_____ Many people come here from China to study.

_____ Few people are going to China to study Chinese.

_____ Where do you come from?

_____ We are going to the bookstore from the library.

3) NOTES ON GRAMMAR: A Time Word (TW) in Chinese can be placed either before or after the subject, but NOT at the end of a sentence like it is in English.

(TM)+ S +(TW) + (Adv) + V +(O) +(嗎)
===================

今天晚上　你　　　　穿　什麼？ What are you going to wear tonight?

_____ What are you studying now?

_____ I am going to buy a pair of pants tonight.

_____ Are you busy on the 6th?

_____ I am not busy in the evening.

8 Find the traditional character and write it beside its simplified form.

妈 (　) 吗 (　) 谁 (　) 语 (　) 雜 (　)

请 (　) 语 (　) 汉 (　) 谢 (　) 當 (　)

词 (　) 认 (　) 识 (　) 说 (　) 學 (　)

欢 (　) 志 (　) 课 (　) 们 (　)

车 (　) 书 (　) 气 (　) 国 (　)

师 (　) 么 (　) 图 (　) 进 (　)

9 Rewrite the following sentences in traditional characters:

1) 你认识不认识谢老师的妈妈？

2) 他告诉我这是美国地图，那是中国杂志。

3) 欢迎，请进，请坐。谢谢。不客气。

4) 谁说这是汉语书？这是中文画报。

5) 你们的车贵不贵？不很贵。我们的车很小。

## 10. READING COMPREHENSION:

Read the text on page 198 and check the following statements as right(V) or wrong(X):

1) (　) 王老師給帕蘭卡媽媽兩張京劇票。
2) (　) 帕蘭卡媽媽晚上用車。
3) (　) 帕蘭卡穿新襯衫和新裙子。
4) (　) 古波穿一件黑的新上衣。
5) (　) 帕蘭卡從古波家去劇場。
6) (　) 劇場很大。
7) (　) 王老師也在那個劇場。

## 11. Find the correct answer and write the letter in the parenthesis.

(　) 1.　她找什麼？
(　) 2.　那本雜誌很舊嗎？
(　) 3.　王老師有多少學生？
(　) 4.　兩個青蛙 (qīngwā:frog) 有幾條腿(tuǐ:leg)？
(　) 5.　這五枝 (zhī:a measure word) 筆都很好嗎？
(　) 6.　姐姐的襯衫是什麼顏色 (yánsè:color) 的？
(　) 7.　你喜歡穿什麼裙子？
(　) 8.　綠的襯衫是你的嗎？
(　) 9.　這兩張票是誰的？
(　) 10.　我的詞典在誰那兒？

A. 八條腿
B. 兩枝好，三枝不好。
C. 找裙子。
D. 都是王老師的。
E. 不是。
F. 是紅的。
G. 紅的。
H. 很多。
I. 在你朋友那兒。
J. 不，那是新的。

## 12. Write a short dialogue:

A:

B:

A:

B:

A:

## 13. GUIDED COMPOSITION (Word order & Sentence order):

Rearrange the words in each entry to make a grammatical sentence.

Rearrange the sentences in the correct order to make a meaningful passage.

Give an appropriate topic for the passage.

1) 沒有　她　朋友　男　還　現在

2) 銀行　在　工作　<u>王大中</u>　現在

3) 男人　是　一個　這個　我的　老朋友

4) 一個　英語系　<u>丁云</u>　　　　的　是　中國留學生

5) 介紹　給她　想　我　一個

6) 叫　他　<u>王大中</u>　的　名字

7) 去　請　他們　我　　看　京劇　晚上　我想
　　介紹　一下兒　給　他們

8) <u>王大中</u>　<u>丁云</u>　愛　不愛　？

9 )　告訴　以後 (later)　我　你

The correct sentence order: <u>4</u>　　　　　　　　　　　　　<u>9</u>

An appropriate topic:_____.

-67-

## 14. CROSSWORD PUZZLE:

CLUES:

Horizontal:

1) buy a pen
2) go to a restaurant
3) What do (you) wear?
5) go by bus
6) opera ticket
7) how many jackets
8) come tonight
10) Where do (you) come from?
11) Which one?
13) this one(map)
15) America
17) A good shirt is expensive.
18) I don't deserve it.
19) read a book

Vertical:

1) buy a bus ticket
3) Which one do (you) wear?
4) go to Beijing
7) How many (of something)?
8) Where are (you) going tonight?
9) jacket
10) from China
11) Which one (ticket) is expensive ?
12) The child is no good.      13) this one(skirt)
14) very beautiful
16) new shirt
20) Does he come to the library?
21) theater

# LESSON 17

1. Listen and write the correct time: shàngwǔ-AM; xiàwǔ:PM

1)　　　　　2)　　　　　3)

4)　　　　　5)　　　　　6)

7)　　　　　8)　　　　　9)

10)　　　　　11)　　　　　12)

2. Listen to the passage, then choose the correct answer.

(　　)1. 丁云今天 (1) 不很忙 (2) 很不忙 (3) 很忙
(　　)2. 早上幾點她去上課？ (1) 八點三十 (2) 九點 (3) 九點半
(　　)3. 十一點四十五分她去 (1) 上課 (2) 食堂 (3) 宿舍
(　　)4. 下午丁云給誰寫信？ (1) 朋友 (2) 姐姐 (3) 媽媽
(　　)5. 丁云和媽媽去哪兒？ (1) 商店和食堂 (2) 銀行和食堂 (3) 商店和銀行
(　　)6. 晚上她去作什麼？ (1) 看京劇 (2) 看電影 (3) 看書

3. Listen and translate into English:

1)

2)

3)

4. Listen and fill in the blanks:

1) _____ 以後，你_____我 _____ 。　我們_____學習。

2) _____ 我們_____去看_____ ，好嗎？

3) _____ 好了。我在_____你。

4) 對 _____ 起，我晚上有_____ 。

5) _____ 點了？ _____ 一_____點。

5. Practice the following characters:

| | | |
|---|---|---|
| 點 | 食 | 堂 |
| 差 | 分 | 刻 |
| 課 | 以 | 後 |
| 事 | 回 | 跟 |
| 起 | 電 | 影 |
| 咖 | 啡 | 半 |
| 等 | 走 | |

6. Choose an illustrated time for each of the following verb-object phrases: 上課，看京劇，坐車，等車，買票，買電影票

Ex: 看八點五十的電影

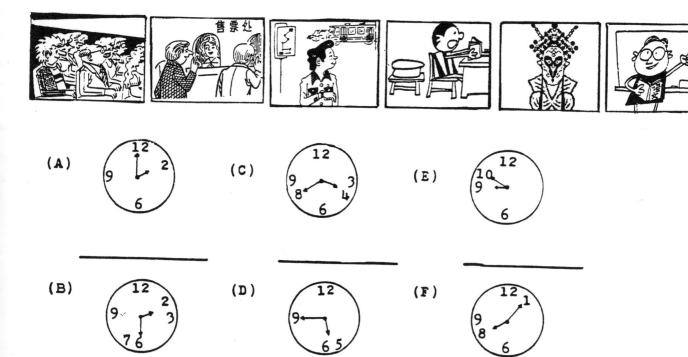

(A)                (C)                (E)

_____            _____            _____

(B)                (D)                (F)

_____            _____            _____

-70-

7. TRANSLATION: Translate the following sentences into Chinese, using the illustrated patterns:

(1) NOTES ON GRAMMAR: 以前 and 以後

A) 以前，以後 and 現在 are all Time Words(TW) and they are placed either before or after the subject, but never at the end of the sentence.(See p.34 現在 )

( 以前 / 以後 )+ S +( 以前 / 以後 )+ V +(O) +( 嗎 )
==================================

以前　　　我　　　　　　　　是學生。 I was a student before.

_____Was she living in China before?

_____He will go to China to  study afterwards.

_____I will work at the bank later.

B) 以前 and 以後 are used after a dependent clause, which is then followed by a main clause.

Dependent Clause 以前 / 以後，Main Clause
=========================
我去中國　以前　，　我學習中文。Before I go to China, I study Chinese.

_____ After studying Chinese, I will work in China.

_____ After meeting him, we often learn from each other.
(We have often learned from each other after we met.)

_____ Before seeing the movie, we go for some coffee，O.K?

_____ After the class is over, what do you usually do?

_____ After class, I go to the dormitory to see my friend.

-71-

8. Translate the following phrases into Chinese, using 對、用、從、跟、給、在、坐、現在、以前、以後 or none of these.

1) Nice to people

2) Say to me

3) Write with a pen

4) Learn from a teacher

5) Come from China

6) Borrow from a friend

7) Lend to a friend

8) Go to the Chinese Department

9) At the Chinese Department

10) Work for a university

11) Wor¹ at the university

12) Buy for your mother

13) Drink tea with my sister

14) Go by bus

15) Write to (my)father in Chinese

16) Before going to China

18) Go to China later

19) Go to China now

## 9. MIND-STRETCHERS:

### 誰是經理?WHO IS THE MANAGER?

張先生(Zhang xiānsheng:Mr.Zhang) 、白小姐 (Bái xiǎojie:Miss Bai) 、
王太太 (Wáng tàitai:Mrs.Wang) 、丁先生（Mr.Ding) 和謝小姐五個人都工作。

這五個工作是電工 (diàngōng:electrician) 、工程師 (gōngchéngshī:engineer) 、
老師、銀行經理 (jīnglǐ:manager) 和大夫。

請問誰是銀行經理？

Clues:

1) 丁先生常跟老師、經理、謝小姐一起去喝咖啡。
2) 王太太的哥哥是工程師。
3) 張先生是老師的好朋友。
4) 白小姐是電工。

Use the following chart to help you figure out who is the bank manager.

|  | 張先生 | 白小姐 | 王太太 | 丁先生 | 謝小姐 |
|---|---|---|---|---|---|
| 電工 | ✗ | ✓ | ✗ | ✗ | ✗ |
| 工程師 |  |  |  |  |  |
| 老師 |  |  |  |  |  |
| 銀行經理 |  |  |  |  |  |
| 大夫 |  |  |  |  |  |

Write the process of your reasoning.

Ex: 1) 白小姐是電工，所以 (suǒyi:therefore) 別人 (biérén:others) 都不是電工。

10. Find the traditional character and write it beside its simplified form:

画（ 　 ）見　　　号（ 　 ）學　　　儿（ 　 ）層
还（ 　 ）現　　　习（ 　 ）漢　　　贵（ 　 ）兒
见（ 　 ）報　　　学（ 　 ）問　　　层（ 　 ）煙
现（ 　 ）還　　　问（ 　 ）習　　　烟（ 　 ）貴
报（ 　 ）畫　　　汉（ 　 ）號

11. Insert a proper measure word, wherever it is required:

那票　　　哪系　　　　那國　　　哪學院

我朋友　　　多少學生　　　這好大夫　　　一宿舍

這裙子　　　幾中國銀行　　　什麼書店　　　一地圖

誰的雜誌　　　這畫報　　　三書　　　一大詞典

多少舊褲子　　　很新的襯衫　　　很貴的車

12. Insert a "的" in the following sentences wherever it is required:

1) 我襯衫是白，裙子是綠。白綠我都喜歡。

2) 很多人從中國來這兒工作。

3) 那件好看大衣是我姐姐。

4) 閱覽室是新；圖書館是舊。

5) 我車不大；他車也不是大

6) 他是很好爸爸；她是很好媽媽。

## 13. GUIDED COMPOSITION:

Rearrange the words in each entry to make a grammatical sentence.

Rearrange the sentences in the correct order to make a meaningful passage.

Give an appropriate topic for the passage.

1) 多　很　事　有　她

2) 以後　下班　王大中，　丁云　找　宿舍　來。

3) 太忙　丁云　但是 (dànshi:but)　今天

4) 看　電影　八點的　晚上　他想　她　請

5) 很　愛　電影　看　丁云

6) 想　很　去　也　她

7) 沒有 (didnot)　跟　王大中　電影　去　看　丁云

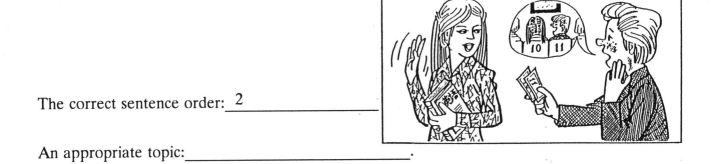

The correct sentence order: __2_____

An appropriate topic:_____.

RIDDLES:

1) 十個加(jiā:add)十個是十個。

　　十個減(jiǎn:subtract)十個還是十個。

　　(Ans:A pair of gloves and two hands)

2) 十個好朋友

　　五個在左 (zuǒ:left), 五個在右(yòu:right)。

　　互相幫助 (bāngzhù:help), 一起工作。

　　(Clue:body part)

3) 有個好朋友，天天跟我走。

　　有時 (yǒushí:sometimes) 走在前，有時走在後。

　　我跟他說話 (shuōhuà:talk), 他不愛開 (kāi:open) 口 (kǒu:mouth)。

　　(Clue: Something that disappears in darkness.)

脸
liǎn

眉毛
méimáo

脚
jiǎo

手
shǒu

# LESSON 18

1. Listen and fill in the blanks:

1) 我 _____ 早上 _____ 起床。 _____ 一會兒書， _____
去學校。 _____ 三十分 _____ 食堂 _____ 。飯後 _____ 宿舍
_____ 。四點 ____ 宿舍到(to)_____ 。 _____ 去 ____ 家。

2) _____ 去書店， _____ 去 _____ 。

3) 他有_____ 襯衫_____ 本子和_____ 京劇票。

2. Listen and write in both Pinyin and characters:

1)

2)

3)

4)

5)

6)

7)

8)

3. Listen to each dialogue, then check the following as right(V) or wrong(X):

1) (　　) a. 丁云去郵局買郵票。
　 (　　) b. 古波想買一本漢語語法書。
　 (　　) c. 古波請丁云給他買書。
2) (　　) a. 他們一起去吃中飯。
　 (　　) b. 丁云五點一刻去找古波。
　 (　　) c. 古波每天都在食堂吃飯。
　 (　　) d. 古波今天沒有課。

4. Listen to each pair of words and the sentence following them.

  A) Write the words in Pinyin;

  B) Circle the word used in the sentence;

  C) Translate the sentence into English.

      Ex: 1)(shàngwǔ)    Do you have things to do in the morning?
              xiàwǔ

2)

3)

4)

5)

6)

7)

8)

9)

10)

11)

12)

13)

14)

15)

5. Listen and answer the questions in either Pinyin or in characters.

1)

2)

3)

4)

5)

6)

7)

8)

9)

10)

6. Practice the following characters:

| 每 | 天 | 床 |
| --- | --- | --- |
| 午 | 飯 | 休 |
| 息 | 時 | 候 |
| 吃 | 題 | 睡 |
| 覺 | | |

Write other characters which have the same component as the one circled in the following characters.

覺:                               床:

時:                               飯:

7. Translate the dialogue into Chinese.

A: On which days do you have Chinese class?

B: I have it everyday.

A: Do you also have class in the evening?

B: No, I work in the evening.

A: You study and work everyday!

B: No, sometimes I visit my friends.

A: Do you go to the library often?

B: Yes, I often go there to borrow books.

A: You are a very good student, I learn from you.

B: Not really (哪里 nǎli), I don't deserve it.

8. Correct the following sentences:

1) 我姐姐喝咖啡，不常在咖啡館 (kāfēiguǎn:café) 。

2) 他們是兩好朋友們。

3) 哥哥從老師來。

4) 少學生學習法語現在

5) 學生沒有多問題有時候

6) 你有沒有很好中國朋友嗎?

7) 我想買兩個襯衫，一是白，一是綠

8) 我喜歡看都中文書和英文書，什麼你喜歡看?

9. CROSSWORD PUZZLE:

PINYIN                    CHARACTER

( )

( )

( )

( )

( )

( )

( )

THE WONDER WORD: _____

Clues:

1) 十二點以前   2) 學生在那兒上課   3) 十二點以後   4) 每天早上都____

5) antonym of 新   6) 學生常常問老師 _____   7) 他們在____吃飯。

**10. Find the traditional character and write it beside its simplified form:**

觉（　）後　　　剧（　）幾　　　个（　）愛

题（　）點　　　张（　）覽　　　写（　）來

时（　）飯　　　两（　）條　　　给（　）筆

饭（　）綠　　　馆（　）閱　　　爱（　）對

电（　）覺　　　条（　）兩　　　银（　）寫

后（　）襯　　　杂（　）劇　　　对（　）紙

点（　）舊　　　阅（　）當　　　来（　）給

绿（　）題　　　览（　）雜　　　纸（　）個

衬（　）時　　　当（　）館　　　笔（　）銀

旧（　）電　　　几（　）張　　　买（　）買

**11. Rewrite the following sentences in traditional characterss:**

1) 这件旧衬衫和那条绿裤子是谁的？

2) 你们去买什么笔和纸？

3) 看电影以后，我给妈妈写家信。

4) 王老师从中国来这儿教汉语，也学习英语。

5) 阅览室有几本杂志和词典？你们有几个汉语老师？

-82

# LESSON 19

1. Listen and translate into English:

1)

2)

3)

4)

5)

2. Listen and choose the appropriate illustration:

1) yìxiē-some

a

b

2)

a

b

3)

a

b

4) lèi-tired

a

b

3. Listen to the story and check the following statements as right(V) or wrong(X):

(    )(1) Zhang enjoys listening to other people's singing.

(    )(2) Zhang sings well.

(    )(3) That person likes to listen to Zhang's singing.

(    )(4) Zhang wants to go to that person's place to sing for him everyday.

(    )(5) The table belongs to Zhang.

Notes: zhǐyǒu - only

      zhuōzi - table

      yòu - again

      biérén - other people

4. Listen to the following paired words,then

(1) Write them in Pinyin;

(2) Circle the word which is used in the sentence;

(3) Translate the sentence into English.

1)  Ex:

 (duō xiě) duō xiè    To learn Chinese, one must write a lot and read a lot, right?

2)

3)

4)

5)

6)

7)

8)

9)

10)

11)

12)



13)



14)



15)



5. Listen and give each of the following statements an appropriate reponse in Pinyin:
(Pay attention to the Chinese etiquette.)

1)

2)

3)

4)

5)

6. Listen and fill in the blanks:
1) 我 _____ 聽 _____ 音樂和 _____ _____ 音樂。

2) 請 _____ 他給我們_____一個美國 _____ 。

3) _____ 告訴他喜歡_____。

4) 你 _____ 紅茶_____花茶？

7. Practice the following characters:

| | | |
|---|---|---|
| 要 | 服 | 務 |
| 員 | 喜 | 花 |
| 紅 | 桔 | 水 |
| 杯 | 瓶 | 讓 |
| 啤 | 酒 | 聽 |
| 民 | 歌 | 古 |
| 音 | 樂 | 代 |
| 唱 | 別 | |

Write the characters which have the same component as the one circled in each of the following characters. Include also characters from the previous lessons.

唱 :                    欠:

話 :                    紅:

酒 :                    服:

代 :                    花:

8. Fill in the blanks with the correct measure words:
1) 我要一____咖啡，　你要几____啤酒？
2) 這____畫報是你的嗎？　那____是我的。
3) 他有多少____地圖和几____新筆？
4) 我們學寫一百____漢字，也學唱三____中國歌。
5) 你有几____唱片？　我有七____。
6) 媽媽給我買一____褲子和一____裙子。
7) 哪____詞典是你的？　兩____都是我的。

-86-

9. Find the correct answer for each question and write down the number:

( ) 1)　你喜歡古典音樂還是現代音樂？
( ) 2)　你要多少唱片？
( ) 3)　你為什麼 (wèishénme:why) 不喝啤酒？
( ) 4)　你要喝紅茶還是喝桔子水？
( ) 5)　這個學生買多少詞典？
( ) 6)　他請我們聽什麼？
( ) 7)　你喜歡什麼水果 (shuǐguǒ:fruit)？
( ) 8)　請你唱一個中國歌，好嗎？
( ) 9)　你看不看中文雜誌？
( )10)　借用一下兒你的車，好嗎？

1. 爸爸不讓我。
2. 都不要。
3. 兩個都喜歡。
4. 兩張。
5. 對不起，我不會。
6. 不常看。
7. 對不起，我今天要用。
8. 我都不喜歡。
9. 中國民歌。
10.很多本。

10. TRANSALTION: Translate the following sentences, using the illustrated patterns.

NOTES ON GRAMMAR: Alternative Question　"是…還是…"：

This type of question is used to inquire about choices or a comparison.

1) Two sentences joined by　還是：

Note that　"是"　can be deleted.

( 是 ) Sentence 1+　還是 + Sentence 2 ?
=====================

　是你去　　　還是　　　他來? Are you going or is he coming?

_____Who buys flowers, the elder or the younger brother?

_____Which one is bigger, China or America?

_____Which one is prettier, the red one or the green one?

_____Which one is better to drink( 好喝 ),
beer or white wine?

_____Who is drinking coffee, you or her?

-87-

2) Choices between predicates with the same subject:

Note that 是 can be deleted, if it is not the main verb.

S +( 是 )+Predicate 1+ 還是 +Predicate 2 ?

========================

你 是 去看電影 還是 回家? Are you going to see a movie or go home?

_____ Is this classic or modern music?

_____ Do you study or work?

_____ Are you American or English?

11. Choose an appropriate description for each of the illustrations.

1) 老師教法語語法。

2) 老師問學生問題。

3) 這個學生每天晚上去看電影，
   現在他睡覺了。

4) 兩點了，上課了，老師來了。

5) 老師說：上課了！
   別說話(shuōhuà:talk) 了！

## 12. READING COMPREHENSION: 這個不能吃 THIS IS NOT EDIBLE

司先生會説漢語，但是不認識漢字。有一天，他肚子餓了，他去一家中國飯店吃飯。

司先生坐下以後，飯店服務員給他一張菜單，對他説："先生，請您看看菜單。您要吃什麼，請告訴我。"司先生看看菜單，他一個字也不認識。他用筆在菜單上畫了一下兒，説："我要這個！"服務員給他一杯咖啡。

司先生喝了咖啡以後，肚子還很餓。他又用筆在菜單上畫了一下兒，對服務員説："我還要這個！"服務員給他一杯茶。

司先生喝了咖啡和茶以後，還非常餓。他想哪個字是菜名呢？大字一定是菜名。他用筆在菜單上畫了最大的那五個字，他想現在一定有好菜吃了。誰知道那個服務員看看菜單，對他説："先生，對不起，這個…這個…，您不能吃啊！"

vocabulary:

肚子 dùzi: stomack; 餓 è: hungry; 菜單 càidān: menu; 又 yòu: again;
能 néng: can.may; 最 zuì: most; 一定 yídìng: for sure; 知道 zhīdào: know; 對不起
duìbuqǐ: sorry
了 le A particle indicating a change of status or a completed action.

everything goes as wishes

新中国饭店

| | | |
|---|---|---|
| 炒饭 | 每盘 | $2,50 |
| 炒面 | 每盘 | $3.00 |
| 炒牛肉 | 每盘 | $4.00 |
| 炒鸡丁 | 每盘 | $3.50 |
| 咖啡 | 每杯 | $0.75 |
| 茶 | 每杯 | $0.50 |
| 啤酒 | 每瓶 | $2.00 |
| 牛奶 | 每杯 | $1.00 |
| 桔子水 | 每杯 | $1.50 |

\*小费在外

\*服务费在外

問題:

1) 司先生在哪兒吃飯?

2) 司先生用什麼叫菜?

3) 司先生認識不認識漢字?

4) 司先生叫了什麼?

5) 服務員為什麼(why)説"先生，這個您不可以吃啊！"?

6) 你想司先生現在還餓嗎?

## 13. CROSSWORD PUZZLE:

PINYIN                    HANZI

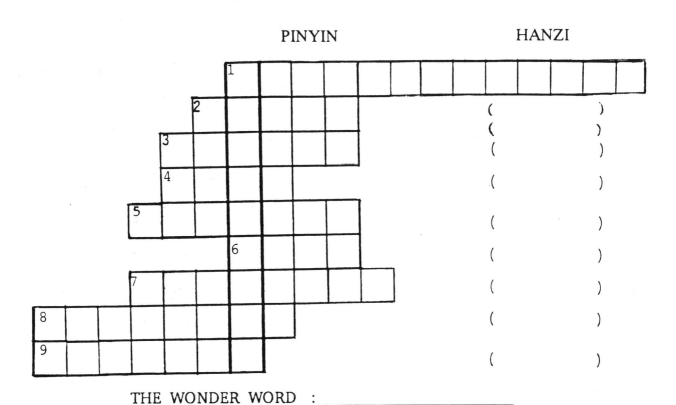

THE WONDER WORD : _____

現代音樂　古典音樂

Clues:
1) 現代人寫這個音樂
2) 喝太多這個以後，別開車 (kāichē:drive)。
3) 茶有小花，中國人喝很多。
4) 外國人喝茶,都喜歡用這個　；孩子都很喜歡吃這個。
5) 外國人都喜歡喝這個茶，茶是紅的。
6) 黃 (huáng:yellow) 顏色 (yánsè:color) 的水果 (shuǐguǒ:fruit)
7) 很多人早上喝一杯，是黃顏色的。
8) 在飯店工作的人
9) 紅顏色的水果

| píngguǒ | lí | xiāngjiāo | júzi | táozi | bōluó | pútao | cǎoméi |
|---------|-----|-----------|------|-------|-------|-------|--------|
| 蘋果 | 梨 | 香蕉 | 桔子 | 桃子 | 菠蘿 | 葡萄 | 草霉 |

## 14. CROSSWORD PUZZLE:

CLUES:

Horizontal

1) not allowing me to drink
2) You sing a folk song.
5) What water
6) no good
7) how much (how many)?
9) Do (you)listen to good songs?
10) Do (you) drink scented tea?
13) Who orders the orange juice?
14) What course does he teach?
15) People are all busy.

Vertical:

1) You are welcome.
2) What wine do you order?
3) know
4) the Han people (the majority of Chinese)
5) What is tasty (good to drink)?
7) drink a lot
8) Isn't wine expensive?
11) good car
12) very few flowers
13) Who teaches you?

16) Is it juicy? (a lot of water)
17) Do you invite him to listen to music?

# LESSON 20

1. Listen to each question and choose the correct answer:

1) a. 十二月　　　　b. 十二個月　　　　c. 是二月
2) a. 三十一　　　　b. 三十　　　　　　c. 十三
3) a. 四個　　　　　b. 十個　　　　　　c. 七個
4) a. 什麼事　　　　b. 一定去　　　　　c. 對不起
5) a. 有意思　　　　b. 沒關係　　　　　c. 什麼時候
6) a. 不大　　　　　b. 很年輕　　　　　c. 二十八歲
7) a. 真好　　　　　b. 沒關係　　　　　c. 是我的
8) a. 謝謝　　　　　b. 對不起　　　　　c. 我沒有唱片
9) a. 祝賀你　　　　b. 生日快樂(kuàilè: happy)　　　c. 是嗎？他幾歲了？
10) a. 幾星期　　　　b. 星期一　　　　　c. 星期幾

2. Listen and circle the word which does not belong to the same category as the other two:

1) 星期　兩年　地址
2) 舞會　音樂會　約會
　　　　　(yuēhuì:appointment)
3) 結婚　英語　漢語
4) 香蕉　蘋果　茶
5) 祝賀　謝謝　問題
6) 通知　告訴　教授
(tōngzhī:notify)　　(jiàoshòu:professor)
7) 知道　事兒　空兒
8) 大夫　襯衫　職員
　　　　　(zhíyuán:clerk)

9) 褲子　杯子　瓶子
10) 實驗室　歷史　閱覽室
(shíyànshì:lab)(lìshǐ:history)
11) 圖書館　飯館　電話(diànhuà:telephone)
12) 愛人　介紹　孩子
13) 紙　吃　唱
14) 休息　學習　雜誌
15) 詞典　字典　唱片
16) 汽車　大衣　裙子

3) Listen to each dialogue and check the statements as right(V) or wrong(X):

Dialogue 1: (　　) A　星期日有時候女人在家寫信。
　　　　　　(　　) B 星期日有時候女人去看京劇。
Dialogue 2: (　　) A　星期五晚上他們去跳舞。
　　　　　　(　　) B 他們星期五沒有課。
　　　　　　(　　) C 他們從學校一起去。
Dialogue 3: (　　) A　帕蘭卡住在大學街。
　　　　　　(　　) B 帕蘭卡的家是 130 號。
Dialogue 4: (　　) A　女人不喜歡音樂。
　　　　　　(　　) B 女人明天下午很忙。
　　　　　　(　　) C 男人和女人一起去聽音樂。

4. Listen to the questions and answer them in Pinyin:

1)

2)

3)

4)

5)

5. Listen and fill in the blanks:

1) ＿＿＿ 我給你們＿＿＿. 你們＿＿＿來＿＿＿三點來？

2) 我＿＿有一個＿＿＿。請你＿＿＿，好嗎？

3) 我們＿＿＿的＿＿＿都＿＿＿。

4) 那＿＿＿很有意思。

有意思　　没意思

5) 你＿＿＿我家的＿＿＿嗎？

6. Listen and circle the date on the calendar:

-94-

7. Practice the following characters:

| | | |
|---|---|---|
| 月 | 日 | 輔 |
| 導 | 空 | 今 |
| 歲 | 祝 | 賀 |
| 舞 | 會 | 年 |
| 參 | 加 | 班 |
| 定 | 意 | 思 |
| 星 | 期 | 知 |
| 道 | 址 | |

Write the characters which have the same component as the one
circled in each of the following characters. (Include characters from the previous lessons.

日 :

意 :

空 :

道 ;

賀 :

址 :

## 8. GUIDED COMPOSITION: Write a note

You see the following announcement posted on the bulletin board of the Chinese department.
Write three notes to communicate with your friend Wang Da-zhong.

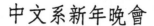

中文系新年晚會

二月三號是中國新年。我們中文系有一個
新年晚會。歡迎老師們 學生們、和你們
的朋友，家人都來參加。

晚飯，老師們給大家作中國菜，請大家來
幫助老師。晚飯以後，有中國古典音樂會
和舞會。歡迎大家參加。

時間：二月三號下午六點
地點：男生宿舍食堂

Note I. You to Da-zhong:

You invite Da-zhong to the party, giving all details about the party.
Do not forget to ask Da-zhong and his girlfriend how they are doing.

Note II. Da-zhong to you:

Da-zhong apologizes that he could not make it due to a prior engagement.

He asks you if you have time to go to a concert on Saturday night instead.

Note III. You to Dazhong:

You accept his invitation and also offer to drive him to the concert hall.

Make clearly where and what time you will meet him on Saturday.

9. GUIDED COMPOSITION (Word order & Sentence order):

Rearrange the words in each entry to make a grammatical sentence.

Rearrange the sentences to make a meaningful passage.

Give an appropriate topic for the passage.

1) 丁云說 跳舞 (tiàowǔ:to dance) 會 (huì:know how to) 不 她

2) 沒關係 她 我告訴

3) 星期三 十四號 四月 生日 我的 是

4) 歲 了 二十 今年 我

5) 舞會 我家 在 一個 有 星期六

6) 請(invite) 我 同學 都 來參加 中文班 的

7) 一定 參加 她 說 她 來

8) 空兒 不知道 同學們 有沒有 但是 (dànshì:but) 我

9) 教她 可以 (kěyǐ:can) 我

The correct sentence order: _3_____7_

An appropriate topic:_____

-98-

10. TRANSLATION: Translate the following sentences into Chinese. using
the illustrated patterns:

NOTES ON GRAMMAR: The QW 幾 is used widely in forming questions. To answer a question
with 幾 , one simply substitutes 幾 with a numeral  The word order remains the same for
both the question and the answer.

1) Asking day and date: Verb 是 is optional in asking the day or the date.

S +( 是 )+ 199 幾年 / 幾月 / 幾號 / 星期幾  ?

========================

今天 _____ 星期幾? What day is today?

_____ What is today's date?

_____ What year are we in?(This year is 199 + 幾 ? )

_____ When (which month,date) is your birthday?

2) Asking age: The verb is not required in asking age.

S +( 十 / 二十 / 三十 /....)+ 幾 + 歲了  ?

========================

你 十 _____ 幾 歲 了 ? How old are you (between 10 & 20) ?

_____ How old is your sister(30 plus)?

_____ How old is your mother(60 plus)?

3) Asking time or date: 現在幾點了? (What time is it now?)

  Note that a Time Word containing 幾 is usually placed after the subject.

S + 幾月 / 幾號 / 星期幾 + V + O ?

====================

你 幾 月 _____ 去中國 ? Which month are you going to China?

_____ On which days do you have Chinese class?

_____ Which day (of the week) are you going to the ball?

## 11. CROSSWORD PUZZLE:

CLUES:

Horizontal:

1) address
2) old people
4) They are nice.
5) to participate
6) Who is seeing him off?
7) Who likes him?
8) I congratulate you (plural).
11) (dancing party) ball
12) noon
17) The son is not there.
18) What time is it now?
19) certainly
20) Are (you) going back or not?
21) Is the classmate in?
23) Whom are (you) welcoming?

Vertical:

1) map
2) Is the teacher in or not?
3) Which class are you in?
4) How old (under 10) is he?

9) They know.
10) Are there a lot of people?
12) high school
13) The lunch is good.
14) Who is that?
15) Sunday
16) spare time
22) to coach

# LESSON 21

1. Listen to each question and circle the correct answer:

1) a. b.   2) a. b.   3) a. b.   4) a. b.   5) a. b.   6) a. b.

7) a. b.   8) a. b.   9) a. b.   10) a. b.   11) a. b.   12) a. b.

2. Listen and fill in the blanks:

1) 今天是帕蘭卡的 _____ ， _____ 同學很多， _____ ， _____ 女的，大家都 _____ 她 _____快樂 (kuàilè:happy). 丁雲____帕蘭卡____ 非常 _____，帕蘭卡_____ 。

2) 布朗先生 _____ 布朗太太 ____ 很 _____ 。布朗先生 還 _____ 丁云 _____ 。

3) 布朗太太 _____ 丁云 _____ 一位 _____日本姑娘。他們____很多 _____ 照片。

3. Listen to the dialogue and check the following statements as right(V) or wrong(X):

(　　) 1. 張太太給她自己 (tā zìjǐ:herself) 買筆。
(　　) 2. 張太太的孩子很高興有一枝新筆。
(　　) 3. 張太太買了兩枝十五塊錢 (kuàiqián:dollar) 的筆。
(　　) 4. 張太太的孩子想買一輛 (a MW for vehicle) 新汽車(qìchē=chē)。

Note:　　不一定- not necessarily

4. Listen and match each dialogue to the appropriate illustration.
　　Choose a or b.

-101-

## 5. Practice the following characters:

| | | |
|---|---|---|
| 束 | 送 | 真 |
| 非 | 感 | 高 |
| 興 | 輕 | 跳 |
| 吧 | 姑 | 娘 |
| 漂 | 亮 | 更 |
| 象 | 開 | 門 |

Write the characters which have the same component as the one circled in each of the following characters.

姑 :

漂 :

跳 :

感 :

## 6. MAKE SENTENCES:

NOTES ON GRAMMAR: As a rule of Chinese word order, all modifiers precede the words which they modify. Furthermore, when an adjective (more than one character), a verb phrase, or a sentence (modifying clause) is used to modify a noun, a 的 must be used after the modifier. The function of the 的, in this case, is the same as that of an English relative pronoun(which,that,who...), which connects a modifier and the noun it modifies. However, note that a Chinese modifying clause PRECEDES, not follows the noun it modifies.

| CHINESE | ENGLISH |
|---|---|
| M.Clause + 的 + N | N + Relative Pro. + M.Clause |
| 我穿 的 襯衫 | the shirt which I wear |
| ("我穿"precedes"襯衫") | ("I wear" follows" the shirt.) |

1) Choose an appropriate modifying clause from Column A to modify a noun in each of the sentences from Column B. Write down the complex sentence .

2) Translate the complex sentences you have made into English.

(A)

上星期從圖書館借的
朋友送給我的
在銀行工作的
王老師今天教的
以前常常去的
參加生日舞會的
從中國來的

(B)

你認識那個姑娘嗎？
我去還雜誌和書。
讓丁云給我們介紹一下兒電影。
禮物太多了。
同學真多。
語法很有意思。
我們去咖啡館坐坐吧！

有意思　　沒意思

(1)

我去還上星期從圖書館借的雜誌和書。

I am going to return the magazine and book which I borrowed from the library last week.

(2)




(3)




(4)




(5)




(6)




(7)

7. TRANSLATION: Translate the following sentences, using the illustrated patterns.

1) Modifying clause+ 的 +S+Adv+V/SV+(O)+( 嗎)
========================================

___我姐姐買 的 花 真 漂亮。___ The flowers my sister bought are really pretty.

_____ The teacher who coaches us is from Beijing ( 北京).

_____ Who is that girl who is dancing with your brother?

_____ The book which you lent me is very interesting.

_____ Are people who drink everyday very happy?

2) S+Adv+V+ Modifying clause+ 的 +O+( 嗎)
========================================

___他 開 他跟朋友借 的 車。___ He drives the car which he borrowed from his friend.

_____ Does she like the young man who works at the bank?

_____ Please lend me the magazine which you read last year.

_____ I like to listen to the song you sang this evening.

_____ Why( 為什麼) don't you drink the wine you ordered?

## 8. CROSSWORD PUZZLE:

PINYIN                                          CHARACTER

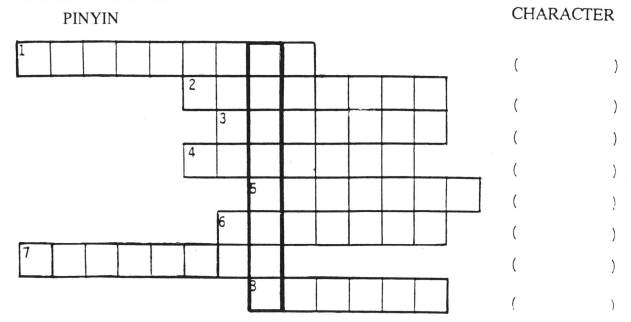

(      )

(      )

(      )

(      )

(      )

(      )

(      )

(      )

THE WONDER WORD:_____

CLUES: 1) 好看  2) 很  3) 別人送你禮物，你很＿＿＿＿。 4) 女孩子
5) 客人來的時候，你說 ＿＿＿＿＿ 。 6) 不是明天，不是昨天。
7) 一張紙，紙上有你朋友，你想他，常常看。 8) 謝謝  (zuótiān:yesterday)

9. Find the appropriate description and write the number under each illustration.

(   )         (   )         (   )         (   )

1. 小明去告訴他的朋友老人給他糖的事兒。小朋友都去跟老人說他的花
真漂亮。

2. 老人的糖都給小朋友了。沒有糖了，現在他去商店要買更多的糖給小朋友。

3. 老人聽了小明說他的花漂亮，太高興了。他給小明糖吃。

4. 小明對老人說：＂你的花真漂亮啊！＂

## 10. READING COMPREHENSION:

### 誰跟老頭子結婚！WHO WANTS TO MARRY AN OLD MAN!

老張和老王是老朋友。老張有一個兒子，叫小明。老王有一個女兒，叫小紅。小明和小紅常常在一起玩 (wán:play)。

有一天，老張對老王説："你看，小明和小紅天天在一起玩。以後他們兩個要是 (yàoshi:if) 能 (néng;can) 結婚，那真好啊！"

老王聽了老張説這個，非常不高興。　他説："老張，你説這個，你這是什麼意思？你的兒子今年四歲，我的女兒今年兩歲。小明比 (bǐ:than)小紅大一倍（大 yíbèi:twice as old)。你不想想，二十年以後，小紅二十二歲的時候，小明不是四十四歲了嗎？你不是要我女兒跟一個老 頭子 (lǎotóuzi:old man)　結婚嗎？"

QUESTIONS:

1) 老王為什麼想二十年以後，小明是四十四歲？

2) 小明二十年以後是多少歲？

RIDDLE　謎語：

像我比我小，有口 (kǒu:mouth) 不説話。

有時 (yǒushí:sometimes) 跟我住，有時在朋友家。
　(Clue: A thing)

# LESSON 22

1. Listen and translate into English:

1)

2)

3)

4)

5)

6)

7)tíngchēchǎng- parking lot

8)

9)chéngxī-west part of the city

10)

2. Listen and locate the places. Write them in characters.

( 京劇院 )

xuéxiaò-school

北京大學

北 běi

西北     東北

西 xī     東 dōng

西南     東南

南 nán

3. Listen to the dialogue and locate each room from the diagram.

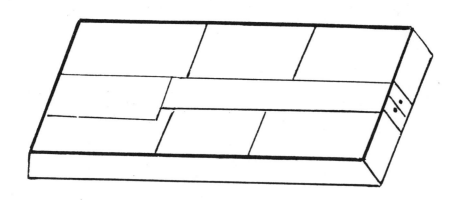

4. CROSSWORD PUZZLE:

PINYIN                                                    CHARACTER

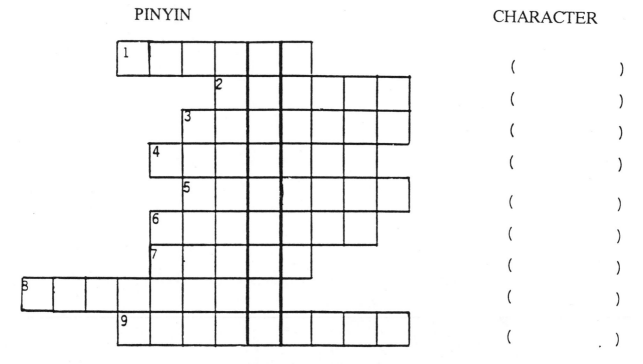

(          )

(          )

(          )

(          )

(          )

(          )

(          )

(          )

(        .  )

THE WONDER WORD: _____

Clues:

1) 人住在這個裡邊。      2) 客人來的時候，你請他在這兒坐。

3) 吃飯的房間        4) antomym of 前面

5) 每天媽媽都要_____房間。 6) 那兒有很多花，在房子的外邊。

7) 人每天要作這個，用很多水。

8) 左邊和右邊是_____。 9) 中國人以前想中國在_____。

5. Practice the following characters.

| | | |
|---|---|---|
| 邊 | 廳 | 願 |
| 房 | 聽 | 裡 |
| 旁 | 椅 | 桌 |
| 總 | 整 | 理 |
| 廚 | 面 | 幫 |
| 助 | 餐 | 左 |
| 間 | 臥 | 洗 |
| 澡 | 怎 | 樣 |

Write the characters from    previous lessons which contain the same component as the
one circled in the following characters.

桌:                          洗:

間:                          邊:

6. TRANSLATION: Translate the following sentences into Chinese, using the illustrated patterns.
NOTES ON GRAMMAR: Words of locations - Always keep in mind that a modifier in Chinese
always precedes the noun it modifies, then you will not be confused with the following
word order.

LOCATION as a modifier of a NOUN: 上邊的桌子 the top table (the table on top)
NOUN as a modifier of a LOCATION: 桌子（的）上邊 the table's top (on the table)

Note that the 的 after the noun as a modifier of a location is optional.

Location + 的 + S+Adv+ SV/V + ( 嗎 )
========================

_____ Is the chair on the left high( 高 )?

_____ _____ The garden on the right has lots of flowers.

_____ The house on the opposite side is very expensive.

S + V + Location + 的 + O + 嗎 ?
========================

我 去 下邊的 咖啡館 。
_____ I am going to the cafeteria downstairs.

_____ Do you want to buy the books that are on the top?

_____ I like the house across the street.

S + V + N +( 的 )+ location + ( 嗎 )
========================

他 去 教室 ( 的 ) 前邊 。
_____ He goes to the front of the classroom 。

_____ Do you like to live in the city?

In the following passage, there are 17 optional 的s, including those
you have learned in    previous lessons. Cross out all the optional 的s.

　我的家住在一個大學的旁邊。我們的房子不很大。左邊的臥室是我的
爸爸和媽媽的；右邊的是我的。我跟我的女朋友住在這間臥室的裡邊。
　我的臥室的裡邊有一張床和一張很大的桌子。桌子的上邊有一張我和
我的女朋友的照片。小花是我的最好 (zuìhǎo:best) 的朋友。她每天總是
跟我在一起。有的時候，她在我的前邊跳；有的時候，她在我的後邊叫；
有的時候 我學習中文，小花想真沒有意思，就 (jiù:then) 在床的旁邊的
桌子的下邊睡覺。小花不會整理房間，但是 (dànshi:but) 他會送(deliver)
報。每天的報，她都送到(sòngdào:deliver to) 我的床的前邊。

NOTES ON GRAMMAR: Words of location are often used with verbs 在, 有 and 是.
在 indicates the LOCATION of a definite object, while 有 and 是 indicate EXISTENCE.

Compare: 哪兒有好飯館？ (Where is there a good restaurant?)
　　　　 那個好飯館在哪兒？ (Where is that good restaurant?)

S + 在 + location/哪兒
================

他的照片　在　報　上。 His picture is in (on) the newspaper.
_____

_____ My sister is in the flower shop.

_____ Who is in front of the table?

_____ Where is China?

_____ Where is your teacher ?

Location + 有 / 是 + object/place
==================

桌子下邊　有　　一本書。 There is a book under the table.
_____

_____ To the right side of the house is a garage. (車房)

_____ Is there a table in the kitchen?

_____ In back of the bedroom there is a bathroom.

_____ Where is there a good university?

_____ There is a garden in the back.

## 7. MIND-STRETCHERS:　怎麼搬家? HOW DID THEY MOVE?

　　小王是一個作家 (zuòjiā:writer). 他愛看書，也愛寫小説 (xiǎoshuō:novel)。
有一個愛唱歌的小謝住在小王家的右邊；還有一個愛請客(qǐngkè:
have company) 的老張住在小王家的左邊。小謝每天都學習唱歌。
老張家每天都有朋友來喝酒，聽現代音樂。小王住在小謝和老張
兩家的中間，沒有一天能 (néng:can) 安靜地(ānjìngde:quietly)工作。

　　有一天，小王對小謝和老張説：“你們兩個人，一個愛唱歌，
一個愛喝酒，請客和聽音樂。那都是非常有意思(yǒuyìsi:interesting)
的事。但是 (dànshi:but) 我是一個作家，作家要安靜地想。你們每天
唱歌，聽音樂，我不能安靜地想，也不能安靜地寫書。我想給你們每
人五百塊錢 (wǔbǎi kuàiqián:$500)，請你們找房子搬家(bānjiā:move)，
好嗎?"小謝和老張聽了小王説這個，都非常高興，兩個人都説:
“太好了！沒問題，我們明天搬家。”

　　第二天 (dì'èr tiān:next day)，小謝和老張都搬家了，但是小王還是
聽見 (tīngjiàn:hear) 小謝唱歌，老張聽現代音樂。他還是不能安靜地
工作。

請問這是爲什麼(wèishénme:why)？你想小謝和老張搬去哪兒了？
他們找新房子了嗎？

## 8. CROSSWORD PUZZLE:

CLUES

Horizontal:

1) Is there a garden in the back?
2) bedroom
3) people on the top
6) in front of the table
7) Who is tall?
8) which side?
9) teach who?
13) outside the reading room
14) big dining room
15) people on the right
16) not very big
18) Good books are all very expensive.
19) how many copies (of books)?

Vertical:

1) The rear bedroom is very big.
3) Books on the top
4) There are people inside.
   (Some people are inside.)
5) Which table is high?
8) Which piece of paper is good?
9) inside the classsroom
10) no children
11) park
12) Japan
14) in front of the gate
17) living room

9. Fill in the blanks with position words:

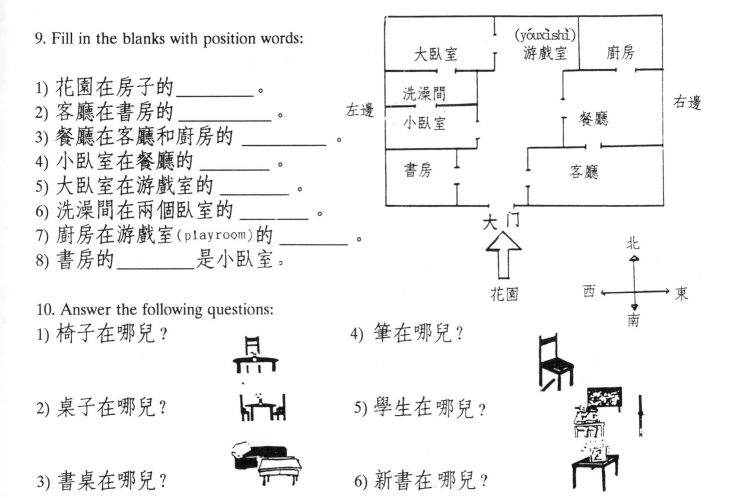

1) 花園在房子的＿＿＿＿＿。
2) 客廳在書房的＿＿＿＿＿。
3) 餐廳在客廳和廚房的＿＿＿＿＿。
4) 小臥室在餐廳的＿＿＿＿。
5) 大臥室在游戲室的＿＿＿＿。
6) 洗澡間在兩個臥室的＿＿＿＿。
7) 廚房在游戲室(playroom)的＿＿＿＿。
8) 書房的＿＿＿＿是小臥室。

10. Answer the following questions:

1) 椅子在哪兒？

2) 桌子在哪兒？

3) 書桌在哪兒？

4) 筆在哪兒？

5) 學生在哪兒？

6) 新書在哪兒？

11. GUIDED CONVERSATION:

Wang wants to borrow Liu's car for two days. Liu can lend his car to Wang for only one day, because he has to drive his friend to the airport tomorrow morning at nine.

Write a dialogue between Liu and Wang.

# LESSON 23

1. Listen and translate into English:

l)

2) xiaōxi-news

3)

4)

5)

2. Listen and choose the correct answer:

1) a.　　2) a.　　3) a.　　4) a.　　5) a.　　6) a.

　　b.　　　　b.　　　　b.　　　　b.　　　　b.　　　　b.

7) a.　　8) a.　　9) a.　　10) a.　　11) a.　　12) a.

　　b.　　　　b.　　　　b.　　　　b.　　　　b.　　　　b.

3. Listen and fill in the blanks:

1) 他們在_____ 工廠嗎？

2) 下____我給他們 ____ _____ 的時候，他正 _____ 呢。

3) 我們_____去吃 ____ 的餐 ____ 在 _____ 的 _____ 。

4) 告____我今____有什麼好 _____ ？

5) 學生看太多 _____ ，沒有 _____ _____ 課文。

4. Listen to each passage and answer the questions in Pinyin:
1) a.
   b.
2) a.
   b.
3) a.
   b.
3) a.
   b.
4) a.
   b.
5) a.
   b.

5. Listen to each pair of words and the sentence following them.
A)Write the words in Pinyin;B)Circle the word used in the sentence;C)Translate the sentence into English.
1)

2)

3)

4)

5)

6)

7)

8)

9)

10)

6. Listen to the dialoques and check the following statements as right(V) or wrong(X):

Dialogue I: (　) 丁云明天從中國來。

(　) 他們明天去接丁云。

(　) 男人下午一點半來接帕蘭卡。

Dialogue II: (　) 古波和丁云的照片在報上。

(　) 代表團訪問工廠。

(　) 古波給丁云介紹代表團。

7. Practice the following characters:

| | | |
|---|---|---|
| 正 | 視 | 接 |
| 話 | 復 | 聞 |
| 表 | 團 | 觀 |
| 廠 | 訪 | 照 |
| 片 | 打 | 明 |
| 城 | 玩 | 出 |
| 發 | | |

8. MAKE SENTENCES: Make a sentence to describe the progressive action in each of the following illustrations.

NOTES ON GRAMMAR: Note that the progressive aspect is shown by using

(1) any one of "在 V..." , "V... 呢" , "在 V... 呢"

(2) 正 (in the midst of) can also be added in front of 在 or the verb for emphasis.

哥哥和弟弟在看電視
( 呢)。

Two actions: One is in progress while the other one takes place.

老師來的時候，
她正在打字 (dǎzì:to type) 呢 。

9. Find the common component of each group of words and write it in the parenthesis.
   From previous lessons, make a compound word from each character.

Ex:
( 礻 ) 祝：祝賀
       禮：禮物
       視：電視

( )  地 城 址

( )  樣 椅 本 相 桌

( )  怎 總 心 感 想 思

( )  好 姑 娘

( )  他 什 們 住 信 你 件 代

( )  綠 紙 紹

( )  沒 漂 洗 澡 法 漢 酒

( )  打 接 把

( )  訪 話 課 謝 談 認 識

10. Find the correct answer:

工人

( ) 1. 你在作什麼呢？
( ) 2. 工人在家嗎？
( ) 3. 那是誰給你寫的信？
( ) 4. 誰想給你買禮物？
( ) 5. 我正在看電視，你呢？
( ) 6. 代表團現在沒空兒，明天呢？
( ) 7. 我用一下兒你的詞典，好嗎？
( ) 8. 請接 829 號分機。
( ) 9. 明天幾點出發？
( )10. 幾點有電視新聞？

1) 不是信，是一張白紙。
2) 愛我的人
3) 不在，他晚上七點回來。
4) 對不起，他們明天也很忙。
5) 複習課文呢。
6) 沒人接。
7) 每天上午十點和下午六點。
8) 我也不知道。
9) 也正看電視呢。
10) 對不起，我正在用呢。

## 11. CROSSWORD PUZZLE:

CLUES:

Horizontal:

1) Please review Chinese.

2) Don't hit him.

3) Answer the phone.

4) The Friendship Delegation is
   visiting the factory.(... 呢)

6) Who does she love?

7) Lend me the Chinese book.

9) The bank is new.

12) I study the new words.

13) The father reads.

Vertical:

1) Please call me, O.K.?

2) Don't pick up (your) friend.

5) Who do (you) represent?

6) Her father works at the bank.

8) Chinese dictionary

10) Who is watching the T.V. news?
    (.... 呢)

11) Which visiting group?

RIDDLE:

一間小房，沒門也沒窗 (chuāng:window) 。
裡邊住了很多人，唱歌跳舞給你看，
每天告訴你新聞。

12. Write two telephone conversations:

(1) To Prof. Xie: You are going to study in China, ask Prof. Xie to write a letter of introduction
(一封介紹信 yìfēng jièshào xìn)

A：喂，...  (Is X home?)

B：請問 ..

A：在，請...  (wait)

C：  (student,so-and-so)

B：我是...  (What can I do for you?
=What is your business?)

C：

B：我想去中國學習...  (study,China)

C：太好了!  (It's great!)

B：您可以...  (Can you give..)

C：  (When,need)

C：明天

B：  (tomorrow,give)

B：

C：

(2) To Xin Hua co.: Ask for repair service for a TV set which you just bought from them.
Suggested vocabulary: 買了 (mǎile:bought)；修理(xiūlǐ:repair)

A：喂，新華公司，您找誰?

B：： _____ (bought TV, problems)

B：_____ (send people to repair)

A：沒有問題。

A：你的地址...
　　電話...

B：_____ (give address,etc.)

B：什麼時候來?

A：_____ (set a time for service)

B：_____

A：不客氣.

# LESSON 24

1. Listen to each question, then choose the correct answer:

1) a.  b.   2) a.  b.   3) a.  b.   4) a.  b.   5) a.  b.   6) a.  b.   7) a.  b.

8) a.  b.   9) a.  b.  10) a.  b.  11) a.  b.  12) a.  b  13) a.  b.  14) a.  b.

2) Listen to the dialogues and fill in the blanks.

1) 你 _____ 有空兒？我 _____沒有課，
我們一塊兒 (yíkuàr:yìqǐ)_____，好嗎？_____！

2) 請問王老師 _____ 嗎？ _____ ， _____ 。

3) 請問 _____ _____ ？ 往前走 (wàng qián zǒu:go straight ahead)，
往右轉(wàng yòu zhuǎn:turn to right), 在 郵局和_____的_____。

4) 他 _____ 話，你都 ____ 嗎？ _____懂， _____ 不懂。

5) 你 _____ _____ ，古波？ 還 ___ ，可是(kěshì:but) 有點累 (lèi:tired) 。

6) 這是媽媽 _____ 作的 _____ 。我_____吃媽媽作的 _____ 。

7) _____ 他今天不 _____ ？因為他 _____ 不喜歡他了。

8) 今天的報紙 _____ ？ 在 _____ 桌子上。

9) 我的書在你_____嗎？ 不在， 在_____ 。

10) 你 _____ _____是誰？ 我 ____ ，是古波 ____ 丁云。

3. Listen to each passage and answer questions in either Pinyin or characters (Give short answers):

1) a.                    b.                    c.

2) a.                    b.                    c.

-123-

3) a.                          b.

4) a.                          b.

5) a.                          b.


4. Practice the following characters.

| 心 | 農 | 村 |
|---|---|---|
| 火 | 鍛 | 煉 |
| 答 | 些 | 難 |
| 念 | 練 | 懂 |


5. Translate the following sentences into Chinese:

1) The questions which the teacher asks in class are too difficult.
Sometimes I understand (them)but I don't know how ( 不會 ) answer(them).



2) Are all of these pictures yours? No, some are mine, some are my friend's.



3) The cookies that she made were very tasty. Everyone who attended the party all loved them very much.

## 6. GUIDED COMPOSITION:

Rearrange the words in each entry to make a grammatical sentence, then arrange the sentences to make a meaningful passage.

Give an appropriate topic for the passage.

A) 知道 她説的話 不是 真的 我

B) 給她 沒有 (didnot) 禮物 買 我

C) 是 昨天 女朋友 的 我 生日

D) 點心 作 給她 我 中國

E) 會 不 作 點心 我

F) 點心 好吃 她説 非常 我作的 可是 (kěshì;but)

The correct sentence order: C _____

An appropriate topic for the passage:_____

## 7. Find the traditional character and write it beside its simplified form:

橘(　) 辅(　) 兴(　) 厅(　) 厂(　)

听(　) 导(　) 轻(　) 总(　) 访(　)

乐(　) 岁(　) 像(　) 视(　) 发(　)

让(　) 开(　) 锻(　) 炼(　) 难(　)

会(　) 务(　) 边(　) 复(　) 练(　)

参(　) 园(　) 团(　) 观(　) 闻(　)

## 8. ANTONYMS:

多 --　　　　上 --　　　　左 --　　　　　　問 --　　　　早 --

這 --　　　　小 --　　　　來 --　　　　　　女 --　　　　以前 --

後邊 --　　　　裡邊 --　　　　起床 --　　　工作---休息

## 9. COMPOSITION:

1) 坐什麼車？

Sugggested vocabulary: 方便 fāngbiàn-convenient; 便宜piányi-inexpensive; 旅行
（lǚxíng）-travel; 貴 -expensive; 舒服 shūfu-comfortable; 來回票-return ticket

2) 學習中文：

## 10. READING COMPREHENSION:

Find the appropriate description for each of the illustrations.

Give a topic for the passage.

TOPIC:_____

(1)小明的爸爸現在有報了。他不看，他還是看旁邊的
那個人看的的報。小明和媽媽都不懂爸爸怎麼
(how come)　這麼(zhème:so)好奇(hàoqí:curious)。

(2)小明快去給爸爸買報。小明給爸爸報，爸爸真高興。

(3)小明的媽媽真不好意思(bùhǎoyìsi:embarrassed)，
她叫小明去給爸爸買報看。

(4)小明的爸爸是一個非常好奇的人。他總是想知道
別人 (biérén:other people) 有什麼，別人在想
什麼，在作什麼。

(5)有一天，他跟愛人和小明在等火車。坐在他旁邊的
一個男人正在看報。小明的爸爸非常想看那個人
的報，他真想知道今天有什麼大新聞。

11. CROSSWORD PUZZLE:

PINYIN                                      CHARACTER

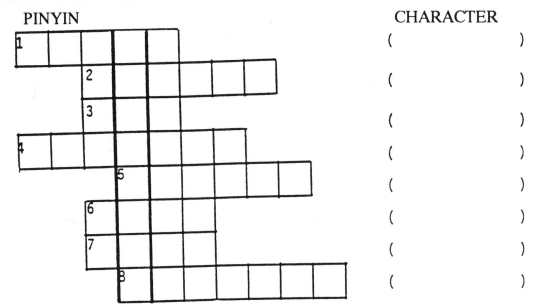

(          )

(          )

(          )

(          )

(          )

(          )

(          )

(          )

THE WONDER WORD:_____

Clues :

1) 學生問問題，老師_____  2) 很長的，在地上走的車。
3) 學習很多，還是不懂。4) 新詞  5) 學習漢語要常常_____ 。
6) 上課的時候，老師叫學生 _____ 課文。
7) 小孩子都喜歡吃這個。    8) 農人住的地方

12. Comment on the picture: 為什麼爺爺 (yéye:grandpa) 奶奶 (nǎinai:grandma)
　　　　　　　　　　不高興？

在中國農村

# LESSON 25

1. Listen to the dialogue and check the following statements as right(V) or wrong(X):

(        )Little Wang has a friend who comes from the United States.

(        )They are going to a Chinese restaurant tonight.

(        )Little Wang's friend has a class now.

(        )Little Wang is going to the library to borrow some books.

(        )Little Wang can't return the books for her friend, because of some problems.

Notes
Dōngláishùn Fànzhuāng
    name of a restaurant
zuì  the most

2. Listen to each sentence and fill in the blanks:

1) 我們 _____ 太晚了，沒有 _____ 停車。

2) 昨天下午古波和帕蘭卡_____到 Billy 家。Billy 作飯_____很好，他請他們吃飯。

3) 古波_____去學校_____很早。他很 _____ 學習。回答問題_____ 得很對，寫字也_____很好。

4) 他的車是 _____ ，他很喜歡_____，他開車_____很____。

5) 星期日帕蘭卡_____同學一塊兒去公園玩兒，玩兒 _____ 很 _____ 。

6) 我每天_____很早， 晚上也_____很早。學習_____認真學習，學習_____很好，休息_____休息_____ 。

3. Listen to each sentence, write them in characters and translate them into English:

1)

2)

3)

4).

-129-

4. Listen to the story once. Then the same story will be told to you again in eight parts. After each part, there will be two questions for you to answer. Answer in either Pinyin or characters. (Short answers)

1)a.                    b.

2)a.                    b.

3)a.                    b.

4)a.                    b.

5)a.                    b.

6)a.                    b.

7)a.                    b.

8)a.                    b.

5. Practice the following characters:

| 得 | 停 | 游 |
| 泳 | 位 | 快 |
| 慢 | 錯 | 面 |
| 河 | 準 | 備 |
| 釣 | 魚 | 湯 |
| 包 | 腿 | 奶 |
| 酪 | 礦 | 泉 |

6. TRANSLATION: Translate the following sentences into Chinese, using the illustrated patterns.

NOTES ON GRAMMAR :

1) Complement of degree after a simple verb:

A verb can be followed by varies types of complements. A complement of degree (CD) is usually an adjective and it is used to comment on the action of a verb. A similar structure in English would be an adjective modifying a gerund.(See example)

The action in such sentences, has either taken place or is habitual.

A "得" must be attached to the verb and also the negative particle 不 is placed before the CD, NOT before the verb.

S + V + 得 + Adv + CD + ( 嗎 )

====================

他 寫 得 很 好 。    He writes well.

_____ (His writing is good.)

_____ The teacher coaches very conscientiously.

(The teacher's coaching is conscientious)

_____ The child doesn't walk fast.

(The child's walking is not fast).

_____ They prepared very well.

(Their preparing was good.)

2) Complement of degree after a verb with an object:

When a verb is followed by an object, then the verb MUST be repeated when using a CD. The 得 is attached to the repeated verb.

Note: Some disyllabic verbs may have a V-O inner structure, and they should follow the same rule as a simple verb plus an object. For disyllabic verbs which do not have the V-O structures, such as 學習 、休息 、歡迎 、介紹 、認識 、告訴 、服務 、喜歡 、知道 、輔導 、整理 、複習 、參觀 、出發 、鍛煉 、訪問 .etc., no repetition is needed.

Following are the verbs with a V-O structure from the previous lessons, DO NOT forget to repeat the verb(the first character).

吃飯 (eat-meal); 上課 (attend-class); 下課 (finish-class); 洗澡(take-bath);
游泳 (swim-swim); 唱歌 (sing:sing-song); 吸煙 (smoke:inhale-smoke); 起床(get up:rise-bed);
畫畫 (paint:paint-painting); 開車 (drive:open-car); 作飯(cook:make-food);
教書 (teach:teach-book); 睡覺 (sleep); 跳舞(dance:jump-dance); 停車 (to park:stop-car)

Ex: 他游泳游得很好。 (right)

    他游泳得很好。 (wrong)

S + V + O + V + 得 + (Adv) + CD + 嗎

=========================

她 作 飯 作 得 很 好 嗎? Does she cook very well?

_____They dance beautifully(美).

_____You sleep too much everyday.

_____I don't speak Chinese fluently yet.


Note that the object can also be transposed in front of the verb or the subject.

In such cases, the verb does not need to be repeated.

When an object is transposed before the verb or the subject， the sentence usually implies a comparison or contrast.

(O)+ S +(O)+ V + 得 + Adv + CD +( 嗎)

=============================

1) 畫兒他 畫 得 好，He paints well,

可是 字 寫 得 不 好。but doesn't write characters well.

2) _____I don't sleep much,

_____but I eat a lot.

3) _____Do you smoke a lot

_____and drink a lot?

4) _____She teaches many new words

_____but little grammar.

# 7. READING COMPREHENSION:

## 誰游得最好? WHO SWAM THE BEST?

三個小孩子在河邊玩兒。他們看見有人在河裡游泳。
第一個孩子説：＂你們知道嗎？我爸爸游泳游得非常好。我看見他在
這水下邊停留 (tíngliú:stay) 了三分鐘。＂
第二個孩子説：＂我爸爸游泳游得更好。他在這水下邊停留了五分鐘。＂
第三個孩子説：＂你們都別説了。我爸爸游泳游得最 (zuì:most) 好了。
四年以前，他從這兒跳下水，　現在還沒有上來(shànglái:come up) 呢！＂

問題：
1) 三個小孩子在哪兒作什麼？

2) 他們説什麼？

3) 哪個孩子的爸爸游泳游得最好？

第一　dìyī  first
第二　dì'èr second
第三　dìsān third

4) 哪個孩子的爸爸游泳游得最不好？

RIDDLES:
1) 有山沒石頭(shítou:rock)
　 有城沒高樓(gāolóu:high building)
　 有路沒人走
　 有河沒人游。
　　　　(Clue:Something on paper)
2) 你走他也走
　 你停他也停
　 太陽 (tàiyáng:sun) 來了他也來
　 太陽走了他也走。
　　　　(Clue: Something that does not exist.)

8. Complete the following two dialogues:

1) Little Wang(A) invites Alice(B) to eat in a Chinese restaurant.
   They order two dishes and one soup.

A: 那＿＿＿桌子沒有人。我們＿＿＿＿＿＿＿＿＿吧！

B: ＿＿＿＿＿＿！

A: 請 ＿＿＿＿＿＿ ！

B: ＿＿＿＿＿＿ 。

A: 你喜歡 ＿＿＿＿＿＿＿＿＿＿＿＿＿ ？

B: 我很喜歡＿＿＿＿＿＿＿＿＿＿＿＿ 。

B: 我聽説這個飯館的 ＿＿＿＿＿＿＿＿＿＿ 。

A: 對了！他們的 ＿＿＿＿＿＿＿＿＿ 。
   我常常來＿＿＿＿＿＿＿＿＿＿ 。

A: 我們叫兩＿＿菜 (cài:dish) 和一 ＿＿＿＿＿＿＿＿ 吧！
                                    (one soup)

B: 太好了。

2) Little Wang meets an old friend Little Zhang(C) and he introduces him to Alice.
They gives compliments to one another.

C: 小王，好久不見了。

(Hǎo jiǔ bú jiàn le:Long time no see!)

A: 小張，好_____.

C: 你好，怎麼樣？　忙____？
A: 不錯，你___？
C: 還可____。(Hái kéyi:so so; nothing special)

A: 來！我___你們_____一_____！
這是我的_____，_____。
這是我的_____，_____。

B:_____！很高興_____。

C:_____！我也很_____。

C: 你的漢語説_____！

B:哪裡！哪裡！(nali! nali!:not realy;

Thank you for your compliment.)

B: 小王是我的小老師，他常常幫助我練習。

A: 不敢當！　我不是_____。
我們互相_____.

-135-

## 9. GUIDED COMPOSITION:

Choose the correct sentence order to make a meaningful passage.

Write 3-5 sentences to finish the composition.

Give a topic for the composition.

TOPIC_____

(1) 你一定都要 (must) 知道得非常清楚
    (qīngchǔ:clear) 。

(2) 你還要 (must) 知道很多事。

(3) 在街上停車也很難。

(4) 在停車場(tíngchēchǎng:parking lot)停車很貴。

(5) 所以 (suǒyi:therefore) 很多人在街上(jiēshàng:on the street)停車。

(6) 從星期幾到星期幾可以停；星期幾到星期幾不可以停。
    從幾點到幾點可以停；幾點到幾點不可以停。

(7) 住在大城裡，停車真是一個很大的問題。

(8) 有時候街左邊可以停，右邊不可以停。
    有時候街右邊可以停，左邊不可以停。

Choose the best sentence order: (A) 7 4 5 3 2 6 8 1
                                 (B) 7 4 3 2 5 6 8 1
                                 (C) 4 5 3 1 2 6 8 7
                                 (D) 4 3 5 2 1 8 6 7

Finish the composition:

Suggested vocabulary: 公共汽車 (gōnggòng qìchē:bus); 坐(zuò:take)
                      開車(kāichē:drive); 貴:expensive
                      錢(qián:money)

# LESSON 26

1. Listen to each conversation twice and choose the correct answer:

CONVERSATION I: Notes:zhè xuéqī-this term;guòqu-formerly

1) Little Zhang    studies :          a) literature  b) Chinese  c) Chinese literature.

2) Formerly，        his teacher taught in:  a) Beijing  b) Canada  c) China.

3) Most of the students are: a) Chinese students b)foreign students c)foreign students from Japan.

CONVERSATION II: Notes: méi jiànguo-have never met

1) Initially Xiaoming wants to invite her friend to come over for supper on

a) Saturday  b) Friday  c) Sunday.

2) Xiaoming's friend can not come, because: a) She has to study

b) She is going to see a movie with her boy friend. c) She has to work.

Who is coming to Xiaoming's place?  a) Xiaoming's boy friend  b) an old friend of her family

c) the boyfriend of Xiaoming's friend.

2. Listen and fill in the blanks:

1) 丁云：帕蘭卡，我 _____ 圖書館借書，你 _____ ？

帕蘭卡：我 _____ 去，我 _____ 借一些 _____ 方面 (fāngmiàn:area) 的書.

丁云：那我們 _____ 一塊 (yíkuài: 一起 ) 去。

帕蘭卡：_____ 現在 _____ 。

丁云：爲什麼 (wèishénme:why) _____ 去?

帕蘭卡：_____ 一個留學生 _____ 我幫助他 _____ 英文。

2) 你 _____ 法語嗎？  我 _____ 不好。

你漢語 _____ 怎麼樣? 我只 (zhǐ:only) _____ 一點兒。

你 _____ 看中文書 _____ ? 我 _____ ，但是 (dànshi:but)  有時候

_____ 詞典。

-137-

3. Listen to the three passages once. Then each passage will be read again and two questions will be asked. Answer the questions in either Pinyin or characters. (Give short answers.)

1) a.

   b.


2) a.

   b.


3) a.

   b.


4. Practice the following characters:

| | | |
|---|---|---|
| 研 | 究 | 早 |
| 談 | 翻 | 譯 |
| 能 | 深 | 解 |
| 或 | 者 | 就 |
| 應 | 該 | 倆 |
| 可 | 容 | 易 |
| 成 | 竟 | |

Find all the characters from the previous lessons which contain the same component as the one circled ⬭ in the following characters.

㴱深:

㴱談:

5. TRANSLATION: Translate the following sentences into Chinese, using the illustrated patterns.

NOTES ON GRAMMAR: Auxiliary verbs

1) 想 and 要 : Both 想 and 要 indicate a mental inclination. 要 is more decisive than 想 . Note that only 想 can be modified by adverbs, such as 很 and 非常.

S +(Adv) + 想 / 要 + V +(O)+(嗎)
========================

我　　想　　喝　一杯咖啡。＿＿＿I would like to have a cup of coffee·

_____Do you want milk in (your) coffee?

_____Would you like to be an interpreter?

_____No. I want to do research in Chinese literature.

_____What would you like to eat?

2) 可以 and 能 : 能 and 可以 are usually interchangeable. 能 may indicate a physical ability, while 可以 is used for permission and allowance.

S + 不 + 能 / 可以 +(PP) + V+(O)+(嗎)
================================
我病了 (bìng le: to be sick)
我　不能　　　　　　上課。 I am sick
　　　　　　　　　　　and I can't attend class.

_____May I smoke?

_____You can't go fishing in that river?

_____Can you teach swimming?

_____Visitors are not allowed to take pictures ( 照相).

3) 會： 會 indicates either (1) a learned capability (know how to) or (2) a future possibility (will).

S +(TW)+( 還 )( 不 )+ 會 + V + (O) + ( 嗎 )

========================

我　　　　還　不　會　説　漢語。 I still don't know how to speak Chinese.

_____ Do you know how to drive?

_____ Will they come tonight?

_____ Will my mother understand me?

4) 應該： 應該 is used to indicate an obligation.

S + ( 不 ) + 應該 +(Adv)+ V +(O)

==============================

(qián)
你　不　應該　　總是　借　錢。 You shouldn't always borrow money.

_____ Young people should work very hard (concientiously).

_____ We should listen to (our) parents' (instruction).

_____ You shouldn't drive after drinking.( 酒後開車 )

NOTES ON GRAMMAR: The use of 就：

The adverb 就 indicates either, an imminent action or has the meaning of "only".

S + 就 +(Aux)+(PP) + V + (O)

====================

我　就　　　回　家。 I am going home right away.

_____ I will call him right away.

_____ They have only one child.

_____ He just takes (study) English courses( 課 ).

NOTES ON GRAMMAR: The use of 可是(but, however)

可是 is a conjunction and it is usually used to join two clauses of contrasting ideas.

Find an appropriate 可是clause for each of the following sentences.

( )1.我很高興輔導你,　　　　　　A. 可是他總是說他很忙。
( )2.這首詩歌寫得真好,　　　　　B. 可是來游泳的人不少。
( )3.學習中文很不容易,　　　　　C. 可是沒有老師能教她。
( )4.這條河的水很深(shēn :deep),　D. 可是他英文說得不好。
( )5.他哥哥想當翻譯,　　　　　　E. 可是現在沒有時間。
( )6.我姐姐要研究英國文學,　　　F. 可是有志者事竟成。
( )7.好朋友應該互相幫助(bāngzhù:help),　G. 可是沒有人瞭解作者的意思。

6. ROD SIGNS:

Fill in the blanks: According to the information on the road signs.

這兒有_____走路，要小心(xiǎoxīn:careful)_____。

前邊的___ 很滑 (huá:slipery), 開車要開得慢一點兒。

有_____在這兒下_____(xiàchē:get off), 要_____。

從星期日到_____,___ _____九點到_____五點，可以
停車停 _____ 分鐘。（從 … 到 : from...to ）

前邊就_____ _____ 。

不_____進去(enter) 。

7. Match the questions with the appropriate answers:

( ) 1) 你理想的工作是什麼？
( ) 2) 你們瞭解郭沫若的小説嗎？
( ) 3) 他的爸爸研究什麼？
( ) 4) 可以請你媽媽介紹一下兒
      中國畫兒嗎？
( ) 5) 學習中文，能加深對中國
      的瞭解嗎？
( ) 6) 你們的大學很有名嗎？
( ) 7) 他是不是你理想的愛人？
( ) 8) 你哪天可以來我家談談？
( ) 9) 學中文很不容易，是嗎？
( ) 10) 明年你會去中國嗎？

A) 現在還不知道。
B) 中國文學。
C) 星期六或者星期天都可以。
D) 我想當翻譯。
E) 對了。很多留學生在
    這兒學習。
F) 對不起，她很忙。
G) 應該可以。
H) 不是，我還在找。
I) 就懂一點兒。
J) 很難，可是有志者事竟成。

8. CROSSWORD PUZZLE:

PINYIN

CHARACTER

(      )
(      )
(      )
(      )
(      )
(      )
(      )

THE WONDER WORD: _____

CLUES:
1) 學很多；   2) 我 _____ 吸煙吗？   3) 從中文寫成(into)英文。   4) 不難.
5) 有志者事竟成是一个 _____ 。   6) 更多   7) 懂

-142-

## 9. GUIDED COMPOSITION:

Rearrange the words in each entry to make a grammatical sentence.
Rearrange the sentences to make a meaningful passage.
Give an appropriate topic for the passage.

1) 漢語　我　太　難　對

2) 竟　成　有志者　事　可是(kěshì:but)

3) 九月　去年　漢語　開始(kāishǐ:begin)　學習　我

4) 練習説　每天　都　中國　朋友　我　跟

5) 以後　中國文學　研究　翻譯　當　或者　想　我

6) 一定　漢語　學好　要　我

The correct sentence order: 4 _____

An appropriate topic : _____

## 10. READING COMPREHENSION:　三句話 THREE SENTENCES

　　有一個外國人就(only)會説三句 (jù:sentence) 漢語 - "太好了!",
"對了。" 和 "沒法子。 (I can't help it.) "。

　　有一天，這個外國人在一個中國飯館吃飯。服務員問他:
"先生，我們的菜好吃嗎?" 他回答説: "太好了!" 服務員説:
"我們的菜也不貴啊!" 他回答: "對了。" 吃飯以後，服務員
看他吸煙，對他説: "先生，對不起，我們這兒不可以吸煙啊!"
他説: "沒法子。" 外國人看服務員懂他説的漢語，非常高興。

　　三天以後，在一個商店外邊，有一個人的車不見了
(bújiàn le:disappeared)。這個外國人對那個人説: "太好了!"
那個人問這個外國人:" 你開我的車了，對嗎?" 外國人説: "對了。"
那個人聽了，很生氣 (shēngqì:angry)，説: "快還我的車! 。你不還，
我要打 (dǎ:beat) 你!" 這個外國人很高興地回答他: "沒法子!"

回答問題:
1) 這個外國人會説哪三句漢語?


2) 這個外國人用那個人的車了嗎?

3) 那個外國人為什麼要打這個外國人?


4) 你想這個外國人的漢語怎麼樣？他應該作什麼?

**RIDDLE**

早上開門，晚上關 (guān:close) 門.
你去看看，裡邊有個小人。

(Clue:A body part)

眼睛
yǎnjīng

脖子
buózi

# LESSON 27

1. Listen to the dialogue and check the following statements as right(V) or wrong(X):

DIALOGUE I:       Notes: Beijing zhōubào-Beijing Review;Wàiwén-Foreign Language

(    ) Today is Monday.

(    ) Yesterday Xiaoying stayed at home and reviewed 12 lessons.

(    ) Xiaoying went to buy something before she and her friend went to a movie.

(    ) Xiaoying bought the Beijing Review at the Foreign Language Bookstore.

(    ) The other person probably will go to the Foreign Language Bookstore this afternoon.

DIALOGUE II:

(    ) They went out for supper.            Notes:zhōngcān- Chinese food

(    ) They chose (to eat) Chinese food.         xīcān-western food

(    ) The daughterr ordered the food.         miàn-noodles

(    ) They had two bowls of soup and one dish.    fàn-rice

(    ) The daughter did not want to drink.

2. Listen to each sentence and check whether the event has been completed or not:

| | 1 | 2 | 3 | 4 | 5 | 6 | 7 | 8 | 9 | 10 |
|---|---|---|---|---|---|---|---|---|---|---|
| Not completed: | √ | | | | | | | | | |
| Completed: | | | | | | | | | | |

3. Listen to each sentence and check the meaning of "meiyou":

| | 1 | 2 | 3 | 4 | 5 | 6 | 7 | 8 | 9 | 10 |
|---|---|---|---|---|---|---|---|---|---|---|
| Not have: | √ | | | | | | | | | |
| Did not: | | | | | | | | | | |

4. Listen to the dialogues and answer questions based on the information given:

DIALOGUE I: a.

     b.

     c.

     d.

Dialogue II:  a.

b.

c.

d.

5. Practice the following characters:

| | | |
|---|---|---|
| 始 | 使 | 招 |
| 嚐 | 茅 | 待 |
| 台 | 爲 | 健 |
| 乾 | 誼 | 康 |
| 葡 | 萄 | 試 |
| 菜 | 筷 | 化 |
| 贊 | 又 | 到 |
| 樓 | | |

6. TRANSLATION: Translate the following sentences into Chinese, using the illustrated patterns.
NOTES ON GRAMMAR: The particle  了, depending on where it is placed in a sentence, can indicate (1) a completed action; (2) a change of status; or (3) an immenent action.

SENTENCE-END  了:
(1) Indicating a change of status: It is equivalent to an emphasized "now" in English.
"  不.....了"means "not.....any more".

我不吸烟了！

S + ( 不 ) +(Aux)+ V/SV + (O) + 了

==============================

我　　會　說　一點漢語　了。　　I can speak some Chinese now.

_____Books are expensive now.

_____I don't smoke any more.

_____I have a car now.

_____He is no longer the ambassador( 當大使).

(2) Indicating a　completed action:

S +(TW)+( 都 )+ V +(O) + 了 + ( 嗎)

==============================

你們　都　　參加　招待會　了　嗎　？　　Did you all attend the reception?

_____He went to China.

_____We all drank wine.

_____Have you tried?

_____All the guests went upstairs.

_____Did you all smoke last night?

上楼来

上楼去

NOTES ON GRAMMAR: Note that a sentence-end 了 after non-action verbs (是， 有，
在，喜歡，好，漂亮，etc) and the auxilliary verbs ( 能，會，應該，etc) indicates only a
change of status.

If the verb is an action verb, then the sentence-end　了 may indicate either a completed action
or a change of status. The meaning of the sentence will be clear only in the context.

Ex:　他吸煙了。 - " He smoked. "　or　"He is starting to smoke."

VERB-END 了:

1) Indicating a completed action, when the verb is followed by a quantitative object(QO).
or a noun phrase.

S + (TW) + V + 了 + QO/N phrase + ( 嗎)

=============================

我 晚上 喝 了 兩杯酒。　　　I drank two glasses of wine tonight.

_____How many glasses of wine did he drink?

_____We saw a very interesting movie.

_____They attended three receptions.

2) Indicating a completed action in an affirmative-negative question.

S +(TW)+ V + 了 + (O) + 沒有?

=========================

電影 開始 了 沒有?　　　Has the movie started?

_____Have you called?

_____Have you tried the Maotai?

_____Have you studied the Chinese culture?

NOTES ON GRAMMAR: 了 is not needed for a past habitual action.

S + TW( 以前 etc)+ ( 常 ) + V + O + 嗎

=========================

我 以前 常 看 電影。I used to see movies a lot.

_____Where did you live before ?

_____I was studying in China last year.

_____He used to have a lot of friends.

-148-

NOTES ON GRAMMAR:　"沒有 Verb" is the negative form of "Verb 了"
and it indicates that a past action has not been initiated.

S + ( 還 ) + 沒有 + V + (O)

==================

我　還　　沒有　　吃飯。　　　　I have not eaten yet.


_____ He hasn't translated this novel yet.


_____ We haven't visited the Language Institute yet.


_____ The movie has not started yet.


7. Match each question with an appropriate answer:


( 　) 1.　他是你們的朋友不是?
( 　) 2.　你几點起床?
( 　) 3.　漢字他寫得怎麼樣?
( 　) 4.　電影招待會幾點開始?
( 　) 5.　你有照相機(zhàoxiàngjī:camera) 嗎?
( 　) 6.　中國大還是日本大?
( 　) 7.　你看了那個電影沒有?
( 　) 8.　學生下課了沒有?
( 　) 9.　你中文説得怎麼樣了?
( 　)10.　你去看朋友了沒有?
( 　)11.　老師説中文，你都懂嗎?
( 　)12.　你游不游泳?


1. 每天七點半起床，
　　可是今天起得比較晚。
2. 下午一點一刻。
3. 我很忙，沒有去。
4. 不都懂。
5. 看了，非常有意思。
6. 很快，可是不清楚。
7. 還不太好。　　(chīngchu:clear)
8. 中國大得多。
9. 還沒有。
10.對了，我們是老同學了。
11.以前常去游。
12.我還沒有，想去買一個。

## 8. READING COMPREHENSION: 日本湯難喝 JAPANESE SOUP TASTES AWFUL

　　有一個中國人在日本參觀訪問。他不懂日文，可是他想日文跟漢字的意思都差不多。他寫漢字，日本人就會懂他的意思了。

　　有一天，他去一家日本飯館吃飯。那時候，他想喝湯和吃飯，他就在紙上寫了兩個漢字 - "湯"、"飯"。飯館的服務員看看漢字，就給了他一碗(wǎn-bowl)水和一碗飯。這個人喝了水，吃了飯，就走了。

　　以後，這個中國人常常告訴他的朋友："你們知道嗎？日本飯 好吃，可是日本湯真難喝啊！"這個人不知道漢字"湯"在日文是"熱水"的意思。

Questions:

1) 這個中國人會日文嗎？

2) 這個中國人在日本作什麼？

3) 這個中國人爲什麼説日本湯真難喝？
　　因爲(because)

4) 漢字跟日文的意思總是一樣(yíyàng-same)嗎？

5) 你想中國人去日本以前，應該學日文嗎？

Notes:

| | | |
|---|---|---|
| 差不多 | chàbuduō | about the same |
| 飯 | fàn | cooked rice, plain rice |
| 熱水 | rè shuǐ | hot water |

9. Quiz on Chinese courtesy:

1) 你請中國朋友去你家吃飯，他們常回答:
　　"太麻煩 (máfán-troublesome) 你了！不要客氣了．"，你應該說什麼？

2) 客人送給你一個禮物，你應該說什麼？作什麼？

3) 吃飯以前，你應該對客人說什麼？

4) 吃飯的時候，坐在你旁邊的中國人總是給你菜，你應該說什麼？作什麼？

5) 你先吃完了，別人還在吃，你應該說什麼？作什麼？

6) 客人說他要走了，你應該說什麼？

10. GUIDED COMPOSITION (Word order & Sentence order):

Rearrange the words in each entry to make a grammatical sentence.

Rearrange the sentences to make a meaningful passage.

Give an appropriate topic for the passage.

A) 中國朋友　給我　介紹了中國大使　我的

B) 參加　去　招待會　中國大使館的　我　上星期六　了

C) 告訴　大使　我想去　英文　教　我　中國

D) 非常　高興　大使　能　認識　我

E) 談話　用　大使　跟　我　中文

F) 我　幫助　他能　找　他說　一個工作

G) 以後　飯　吃了，　看了　中國電影　一個　還　我們

A correct sentence order: __B_____ 。

An appropriate topic for this passage:_____ 。

RIDDLE:

姐姐妹妹一樣高，吃飯時候他們就到。
是鹹是淡一起嘗，少了一個工作不了。　(Clue:A thing)

Notes:　鹹 (xián-salty);淡 (dàn-not salty); 工作不了 (gōngzuò bù liǎo-can't work).

-152-

# 你身體健康嗎？

## 你買什麼？

☐ 你買很多牛肉(níuròu:beef).

☐ 你買很多奶酪和牛奶。
  奶酪。

☐ 你買很多準備好的
  快餐。(kuàicān:fast food)

## 你吃什麼？

☐ 你吃很多炸(zhá:fried))的菜。

☐ 你每天喝很多杯咖啡。

☐ 你吃很多甜(tián:sweet)點心。

☐ 在飯店，你只叫好吃的菜，對健康
  好不好沒關係。

## 你運動嗎？

☐ 你每天都開車。
  坐車上學或者上班。

☐ 你不喜歡作運動。

☐ 你不喜歡走路。

RESULT:

| | | |
|---|---|---|
| 0 | check | 很健康 |
| 1-3 | checks | 健康 |
| 4-6 | checks | 不很健康 |
| 7-9 | checks | 不健康 |
| 10 | checks | 很不健康 |

**Write a short passage about the three meals you eat everyday.**

你每天三餐，都常吃什麼？喝什麼？幾點吃？在哪兒吃？
你也愛吃點心嗎？

早飯

中飯

晚飯

點心

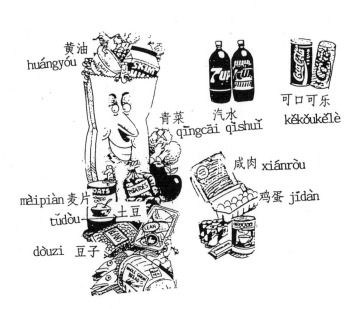

黄油 huángyóu

青菜 qīngcāi　汽水 qìshuǐ

可口可乐 kěkǒukělè

咸肉 xiánròu

màipiàn 麦片

鸡蛋 jīdàn

tǔdòu 土豆

dòuzi 豆子

# LESSON 28

1. Listen and choose the correct answer:

(    )This narration is about a)spring  b)winter  c)summer

(    )This year winter arrived

    a)rather early  b) rather late  c)just the right time.

(    )In winter, a)we  don't have snmow

    b)we often have snow  c)we sometimes have snow.

(    )The favorite winter sports are

    a)football and skiing  b) skating and volleyball  c)skiing and skating.

Notes:
Jiānádà-Canada
wán:finish
xiàxuě-snow
huáxuě-skiing
cháng-long
zuì-most

2. Listen to each question and choose the correct answer:

| 1) a. | 2) a. | 3) a. | 4) a. | 5) a. | 6) a. | 7) a. |
|-------|-------|-------|-------|-------|-------|-------|
| b. | b. | b. | b. | b. | b. | b. |

| 8) a. | 9) a. | 10) a. | 11) a. | 12) a. | 13) a. | 14) a. |
|-------|-------|--------|--------|--------|--------|--------|
| b. | b. | b. | b. | b. | b. | b. |

3. DICTATION: Write in characters and translate them into English:

1)

2)

3)

4)

4. Listen and differentiate the following sentences, whether the event are in the past, future or present.

    1.   2.   3.   4.   5.   6.   7.   8.   9.   10.

| | | | | | | | | | | |
|---------|---|---|---|---|---|---|---|---|---|---|
| future | | | | | | | | | | |
| present | | | | | | | | | | |
| past | | | | | | | | | | |

5. Listen and fill in the blanks:

1) 他去大____館____簽____了沒有？

2) 我想____一 ____ _____ 和一頂 _____。

3) 我們____贏了，十二____八。裁判很_____。

4) 你最 _____ 什麼 _____ ？足____籃____都有_____。

5) _____ 來了。我們可以去_____了。

6. Practice the following characters:

| | | |
|---|---|---|
| 足 | 球 | 賽 |
| 昨 | 辦 | 簽 |
| 證 | 隊 | 贏 |
| 輸 | 比 | 裁 |
| 判 | 公 | 平 |
| 氣 | 踢 | 李 |
| 帽 | 雙 | 頂 |
| 冰 | 鞋 | 冬 |
| 滑 | | |

Write from previous lessons the characters which contain the same component as the one circled in each of the following characters.

帽 : 判 :

踢 : 球 :

隊 : 簽 :

7. TRANSLATION: Translate the following sentences into Chinese, using the illustrated patterns.

1) NOTES ON GRAMMAR: Affirmative-negative question with 了沒有.

An affirmative-negative question inquires whether an action has taken place.(See p.149)

S + V +(O) + 了沒有?
==================

招待會 開始 了 沒有 ? _____Has the reception started (or not)?

_____Have you or haven't you seen the football game?

_____Did you or didn't you buy the skates?

A variation of the above pattern is:

S + V + 沒 + V + (O) ?
=======================

你 贏 沒 贏 ? _____Did you or didn't you win?

_____Did you or didn't you apply for the visa?

_____Have you or haven't you had supper?

2) NOTES ON GRAMMAR: Sentence with sequential actions:

(1) An action had been completed before the second action took place. 就 is used to indicate that the two actions follow closely one after the other. Note that 就 is placed right AFTER, not BEFORE, the subject of the second clause.

S + V+ 了 +(O)( 以後 ),S + 就 +V +(O) + 了
=====================================

下 了 課 以後, 就 回 家 了。After the class was over, I went home.

_____After he had eaten, he went to bed
(right away).
_____After he had watched TV, he left.

-157-

(2) An action will have been completed before a second action will take place.

Note that there is no structural difference between the first clauses of 1) and 2).

S + V+ 了 +(O)+ 以後 ,S+(就 )( 要)+V+(O)

============================

___下 了 課 以後，我 就 要回家。___After the class is over,(then)I'll go home.

_____After eating, I'll go to bed (right away).

_____After watching TV, he'll leave.

_____After studying Chinese, I'll work as an interpreter.

8. COMPOSITION: Topic: 我最喜歡的運動

打排球　打籃球　打網球　打乒乓球　　踢足球　　打棒球

滑冰　　滑雪　　慢跑　　划船　　　游泳

9. Describe what 小明 did yesterday. Use the pattern illustrated in 7.2)-(1)

Ex: 昨天小明起床起
　　得很早。

起了床以後，
他就吃早飯。

吃了早飯，

他就 ……

## 10. CROSSWORD PUZZLE:

CLUES:

Horizontal:

1) go and look for the coach.
2) office
3) sign (name)
4) prove, certify
6) The weather is good.
7) ask the guests to eat.
10) scored
12) skating
16) young people
18) unfair
20) not too cold
21) drink water
15) everyday

Vertical:

1) go to apply for a visa
5) classroom
7) Please come in.
8) delicious(good to eat)
9) annoying, get someone angry
11) understand
13) The ice water is too cold.
14) next winter
17) There are not many good people.
  (Good people are not many.)
19) park

# LESSON 29

1. Listen and fill in the blanks:

1) 加拿大的 ＿＿＿＿＿很冷，＿＿＿＿ 很多。每年 ＿＿＿＿ 十一月＿＿＿＿
三月是＿＿＿＿＿。 但是我和我朋友都 ＿＿＿＿＿ ＿＿＿＿＿ ，
因為我們可以 ＿＿＿＿ 滑雪。

2) 我們一個朋友今天 ＿＿＿＿ 美國 ＿＿＿＿ 看我。我到＿＿＿＿＿接他。我
們以前(before) 在學校的 ＿＿＿＿＿ ， ＿＿＿＿ 去旅行(travel )。
我喜歡＿＿＿＿，他喜歡＿＿＿＿。我們都不喜歡坐 ＿＿＿＿＿ 。
我們已經好多年沒見面 (jiànmiàn:see each other) 了。

2. Listen to each question and choose the corrct answer or response.
1) a   b        2) a   b        3) a   b            4) a   b

5) a   b        6) a   b        7) a   b            8) a   b

9) a   b        10) a   b       11) a   b           12) a   b

13)a   b        14) a   b       15) a   b           16) a   b

3. Write  in characters and translate the sentences into English:
1)

2)

3)

4. Listen to the story once, then answer the questions given in six sections. Answers can be in either Pinyin or characters. (Give short answers.)

1) a.

   b.

   c.

2) a.

   b.

   c.

3) a.

   b.

   c.

4) a.

   b.

5) a.

   b.

   c.

6) a.

   b.

   c.

5. Practice the following characters:

| | | |
|---|---|---|
| 飛 | 機 | 場 |
| 站 | 緊 | 注 |
| 別 | 願 | 離 |
| 忘 | 所 | 步 |
| 努 | 力 | 身 |
| 體 | 放 | 過 |
| 夏 | 秋 | 路 |
| 安 | | |

6. TRANSLATION: Translate the following sentences into Chinese, using the illustrated patterns.

NOTES ON GRAMMAR: Imminent action

A sentence-end 了 ,used with 要，就，快 indicates that a new situation will soon take place.
Among the five variations - 要，快，就，快要，就要，
"就" and "就要" are more imminent than the other three.
Note: 快 and 快要 may not be used together with a time word.

S + 就 / 快 / 要 / 快要 / 就要 + V+(O)+ 了
=============================

飛機 _____ 就 要 起飛了。The plane is taking off    any minute.

_____ Winter will be here( 到 ) soon.

_____ The delegation will (soon) be here at two.

_____ The class will start (soon) at one.

7. Find an appropriate definition for each of the  following words:

(    ) 公園       (1) 飛機在這兒起飛和停。
(    ) 教室       (2) 在外國學習的學生
(    ) 飛機場     (3) 那兒有很多樹和花，大家都可以去玩兒。
(    ) 難過       (4) 很不高興
(    ) 進步       (5) 學生上課的房間
(    ) 裁判       (6) 每天中午吃的飯
(    ) 中飯       (7) 比賽的時候，他說哪隊贏，哪隊輸。
(    ) 洗澡       (8) 以前不好，現在比較好了。
(    ) 簽證       (9) 用很多水洗身體。
(    ) 留學生    (10) 你去外國，一定要辦這個。

8. Write a short passage to describe each of the following illustrations.
Use 了 to indicate a change of status.

-164-

9. Write a short dialogue for each of the following situations.

1)

2)

3)

4)

# 10. CROSSWORD PUZZLE:

**PINYIN**            汉字

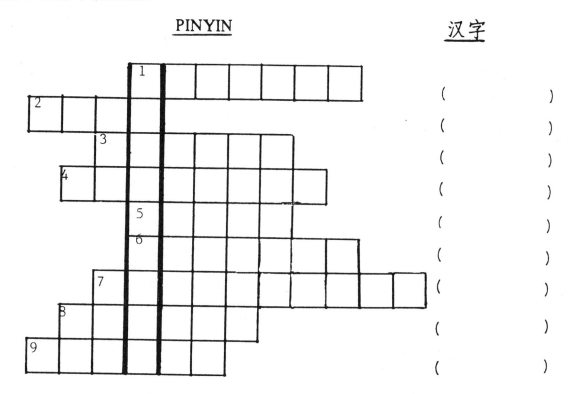

(　　　　) 
(　　　　) 
(　　　　) 
(　　　　) 
(　　　　) 
(　　　　) 
(　　　　) 
(　　　　) 
(　　　　)

THE WONDER WORD:＿＿＿＿＿＿＿＿＿＿

Clues:

1) 夏天以後

2) 學習很多，工作很多。

3) 比賽的時候，他說誰輸誰贏。

4) 去飛機場跟朋友說再見。

5) 很多男人都喜歡的運動

6) 冬天的運動．

7) 飛機起飛或者停留的地方

8) 不在一起了。

9) 心裡不高興。

**RIDDLES**

1) 哥哥長，弟弟短。
          (duǎn:short)

天天比賽大家看。

哥哥跑了十二圈；
   (paǒ:run) (quān:circle)

弟弟跑了只一圈。

(Clue:A thing)

2) 踢他，他跑。

打他，他跳。
         (tiào:jump)

踢他，打他，

他都不叫。

(Clue:A thing)

11. Plan a trip:

   You are planning a trip to a foreign country, find out the following information and make a budget.

1) the itinerary;

2) fares of plane, bus or train;

3) room and board expenses;

4) car renting;

5) pocket money for entertainment
   and souvenirs( 紀念品-jìniàn pǐn)

12. Match each describtion with the appropriate illustration:

A

B

C

D
VISA
MasterCard

1) 你在商店買了東西 (dōngxi:thing) 以後，你用這張
   紙，可以不給他們現錢 (xiànqián:cash). 一個月以後,
   公司給你信，告訴你你應該還他們多少錢。

2) 你買的東西太多了，可以讓商店送到你的家。
   這個服務，你應該給他們一點兒錢。

3) 你沒有空兒去商店買東西，可以打電話給
   商店，告訴他們你要的東西是什麼，商店會
   送東西到你家。

4) 你在報上看見你喜歡的一件東西，你可以寫信
   或者 打傳真 (dǎ chuánzhēn:send fax) 給那個公司,
   跟他們買那個東西。

13. Write a short passage,describing the following pictures.

Suggested words:

| 聖誕節 | Shèngdànjié | Christmas |
|---|---|---|
| 聖誕樹 | Shèngdàn shù | Christmas tree |
| 聖誕卡 | Shèngdàn kǎ | Christmas card |
| 聖誕老人 | Shèngdàn lǎorén | Santa Claus |
| 壁爐 | bìlú | fireplace |
| 襪子 | wàzi | stocking |

十二月二十日是聖誕節。聖誕節就要到了。現在大家都非常忙。

爸爸....

郵差 yóuchāi

# LESSON   30

1. Listen to the passage and choose a correct answer:
(    ) Little Wang would like to      a) go to a movie      b) study
       c) see an exhibition.
(    ) Wang helped his friend to review her lessons      a) after supper      b) after the movie
       c) before supper.
(    ) When did the movie start?      a) 7:30      b) 8:15      c) 8:30
(    ) When is Wang's friend going to see an exhibition?                Notes:
     a) Friday      b) Saturday      c) Sunday                zhǎnlǎn-exhibition
       bāngzhù-help

2. Write   in characters, then translate the sentences into English:
1)



2)



3)



4)



3. Listen to the passage and check the statements as right(V) or wrong(X):
(      ) Gubo and Palanka went to a ball held by the Chinese Student Association.
(      ) Ding Yun sang a Chinese song at the party.
(      ) Ding Yun was going to teach Gubo and Palanka a very easy Chinese song.
(      ) Everyone said that they would sing it well.

4. Listen and fill in the blanks:

1) 請你_____，請你 ____ _____ 了。

2) _____ 就要_____了。別 ___ 了。

3) ___ 了以後，給我來____。

4) 謝謝你熱情的_____。

5) 中國___日本___不___?

6) 學習中文___天都要 _____ _____ 。

7) _____ 我_____給我買了很多_____。

8) ____ 大使的_____乾杯。

9) 我説___不好，請大家不要_____ _____我。

10) _____的事_____作。

5. Practice the following characters:

| 笑 | 東 | 西 |
|---|---|---|
| 哭 | 熱 | 情 |
| 自 | 己 | |

Find the characters from the previous lessons which contain the same component as the one circled in the following characters.

熱:                     情:

笑:

6. TRANSLATION: Translate the following sentences into Chinese, using the illustrated patterns.
NOTES ON GRAMMAR: The preposition 離 (from, to) is used to indicate the distance from place A to place B. It is usually used with SVs 遠 (far) 近 (jìn:near) or the mileage "X 公里" (gōnglǐ:kilometer).
Place A + 離 +Place B +(Adv)+ SV +( 嗎)
==================================

中國　　離　　日本　很　　近。 China is very close to Japan.
_____

_____ The airport is not very far from his house.

_____ Is your dormitory far from the classroom?

_____ The bookstore is not too far from our school.

7. Change the following sentences, using the 離 pattern.

　Ex: 從工廠到宿舍很近。- 工廠離宿舍很近。

1) 從加拿大到美國很近。

2) 從火車站到飛機場不很遠。

3) 從你家到大學遠還是從書店到大學遠?

4) 從中文系到圖書館有幾公里 (gōnglǐ:kilometer) ?

5) 從我家到宿舍非常近。

远 (遠)　　近

VANCOUVER 2000 miles

1 BLOCK TO BENS

8. Correct the grammatical errors in the following sentences:
1)　下課了昨天，就我去看一個電影了。


2)　星期六他來了我家的時候，我正看電視了。


3)　我們常常去了參加足球比賽去年。


4)　去年冬天太冷了，我們沒有去滑冰了。


5)　代表團坐了飛機去中國。


6)　飛機兩點鐘快要起飛。你怎麼還沒有去機場了？


7)　他起床了很早今天。我沒有起的很早。


8)　有時候我看電影了，有時候我釣魚了。


9)　你們明天快要走了，我真難過了。


10)　你吃了飯嗎？吃了飯。你呢？


11)　謝謝你得熱情的招待。不客氣，歡迎又來了。

9. Find the missing 了s in the following passages. Add them in the appropriate places.

1) Nine 了s are missing:

去年夏天 (xiàtiān:summer) 我在一家美國公司當翻譯。每天早上我都起得很早，因為我要坐公共汽車去上班。工作三個月以後，我跟朋友借兩千塊錢 (liǎngqiān kuàiqián·$2,000) 買一個舊車。我想現在我每天都可以開車去上班，每天早上也可以起得晚一點兒。

我第一天開車去上班，心裡太高興。可是下班的時候，我的老板 (lǎobǎn:boss) 告訴我：“小王，真對不起，現在我們公司的工作少，你以後不用來上班。”我聽他的話，心裡真難過。
請問，我跟朋友借的錢怎麼還他呢？真氣人！

2) Six 了s are missing:
  A: “我想去買一點兒東西，你去不去？”
  B: “我昨天買很多東西。不想去，你自己去吧！”
  A: “買東西以後，我要去看電影，你去不去？”
  B: “電影八點就要開始。你沒有時間 (shíjiān:time) 買東西。”
  A: “你説得對。我今天不去買。”

10. Write the antonyms:

| | | |
|---|---|---|
| 1) 送 | 2) 後 | 3) 贏 |
| 4) 難 | 5) 來 | 6) 笑 |
| 7) 早 | 8) 慢 | 9) 上 |
| 10) 裡 | 11) 問 | 12) 對 |
| 13) 高興 | 14) 難看 | 15) 近 |
| 16) 別人 | 17) 這 | 18) 借 |
| 19) 舊 | 20) 冷 (lěng:cold) | |

好看---難看

快---慢

老---小

多---少

來---去

11. Find the simplified form for each of the complicated characters and write it beside its complicated form.

錯（　　）飛（　　）熱（　　）東（　　）緊（　　）

礦（　　）機（　　）賽（　　）氣（　　）嚐（　　）

準（　　）廠（　　）辦（　　）頂（　　）爲（　　）

備（　　）願（　　）簽（　　）雙（　　）乾（　　）

釣（　　）離（　　）證（　　）談（　　）誼（　　）

湯（　　）體（　　）隊（　　）應（　　）試（　　）

譯（　　）過（　　）贏（　　）倆（　　）贊（　　）

輸（　　）樓（　　）

12. Rewrite the following sentences in simplified characters:

1) 飛機場離大使館遠不遠？

2) 你家離圖書館遠還是離大學遠？

3) 我們應該互相學習，互相幫助。

4) 參贊說"爲我們兩國的友誼乾杯！祝大家身體健康！"

5) 東西都準備好了嗎？　上飛機吧！

6) 比賽我們隊輸了。心裡真難過。

-174-

## 13. READING COMPREHENSION:

牛 (niú:cow) 吃草(cǎo:grass)　THE COW ATE THE GRASS

　　有一天，一個畫家(painter)在他朋友家吃飯。朋友知道畫家畫畫兒畫得很好，就請畫家給他畫一張畫兒。畫家說沒問題。

　　一個月以後，畫家的朋友來畫家的家。他問畫家："你給我畫的畫兒呢？"
畫家說："我給你畫了一張很大的畫兒。來，請來畫室看看吧！"

　　進了畫室以後，畫家指着 (zhǐzhe;pointing to) 一張白紙對朋友說：
　　"你喜歡這張畫兒嗎？"
朋友問畫家："你畫的畫兒在哪兒？你畫的是什麼東西？"
畫家說：　"我畫的是牛吃草啊！"
朋友問：　"牛吃草！草在哪兒？"
畫家回答："牛吃了。"
朋友又問："那麼，牛呢？"
畫家回答："草都沒有了，牛還會在這兒嗎？"

回答問題:
1) 畫家給朋友畫畫兒了沒有？

2) 畫家喜歡不喜歡給朋友畫畫兒？

3) 以後朋友還會請畫家給他畫畫兒嗎？

RIDDLES:

你哭他也哭，你笑他也笑。
前邊看見他，後邊找不到。 (Clue:A person)

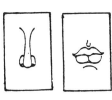

東一片，西一片，
到老不見面。　　(Clue:A body part)

鼻子
bízi

嘴
zuǐ

耳朵
ěrduo

## 14.CROSSWORD PUZZLE:

CLUES:

Horizontal:

1) I am leaving.

2) himself

5) cordial,enthusiastic

6) Don't cry anymore.

8) Are you happy?

9) to take off (plane)

12) camera

13) Good bye

14) sad

16) young

18) Don't laugh.

19) (You) didn't win,(I suppose).

20) thing

Vertical:

1) myself

2) He can't get up.

3) understand you

4) very hot

7) Did (you) win?

10) airport

11) mutual

12) take a picture

15) celebrate New Year

17) the light one

20) There are many Oriental people.
     (Oriental people are many.)

21) very few Caucasians

# 生字表

======

煙　二　七　紹　孩　新　找　跟　睡

吸　層　六　介　愛　相　從　回　題

氣　習　四　見　來　行　互　太　事　候

客　院　號　再　紙　銀　當　上　後　時

誰　謝　外　少　下　去　筆　姐　敢　晚　以　走　息

夫　語　迎　叫　多　用　常　買　妹　口　館　劇　白　課　等　休

都　現　法　店　沒　訴　叫　本　京　綠　刻　半　飯

們　友　大　漢　歡　生　住　現　英　商　了　有　告　几　誌　票　衫　分　啡　吃

也　弟　朋　書　師　圖　進　學　舍　典　識　啊　説　家　信　個　雜　張　襯　差　咖　午

呢　他　媽　她　老　地　您　留　宿　五　詞　一　報　十　認　喂　和　想　寫　系　室　兩　件　堂　影　床

嗎　哥　爸　那　人　麼　茶　問　兒　零　畫　九　先　字　對　工　給　文　覽　裙　穿　食　電　天

好　很　不　是　車　國　什　喝　姓　坐　中　閱　條　舊　點　起　每　覺

你　我　忙　這　的　哪　看　請　貴　在　三　還　八　女　名　男　作　子

別 會 址 漂 面 照 懂 位 就 誼 裁 鞋 緊

水 讓 舞 道 娘 廚 樣 訪 練 湯 者 乾 比 冰 站 安

代 唱 賀 知 姑 理 怎 廠 念 魚 或 康 樓 輸 雙 力 路

紅 樂 祝 期 吧 整 裡 觀 難 釣 腿 解 健 到 贏 帽 努 秋

花 音 歲 星 跳 總 澡 團 些 備 泉 深 竟 為 又 隊 頂 步 夏 己

喜 古 年 思 輕 桌 洗 表 發 答 準 礦 能 成 台 贊 證 箱 所 過 自

小 歌 今 意 興 送 椅 臥 聞 出 煉 泳 酪 譯 易 茅 化 簽 李 離 忘 情

杯 民 空 定 高 門 旁 間 複 玩 鍛 游 奶 翻 容 嚐 試 辦 氣 願 放 熱

員 聽 導 同 感 開 廳 左 話 城 火 河 包 談 可 待 筷 昨 踢 別 體 哭

務 酒 輔 班 非 象 房 餐 接 明 村 前 錯 早 倆 招 菜 賽 平 場 身 西

服 啤 月 加 真 更 園 助 視 打 農 停 慢 究 該 使 葡 球 公 滑 機 意 東

要 瓶 日 參 束 亮 邊 幫 正 片 心 得 快 研 應 始 足 判 冬 飛 注 笑

(19) (20) (21) (22) (23) (24) (25) (26) (27) (28) (29) (30)

# BASIC MEASURE WORDS

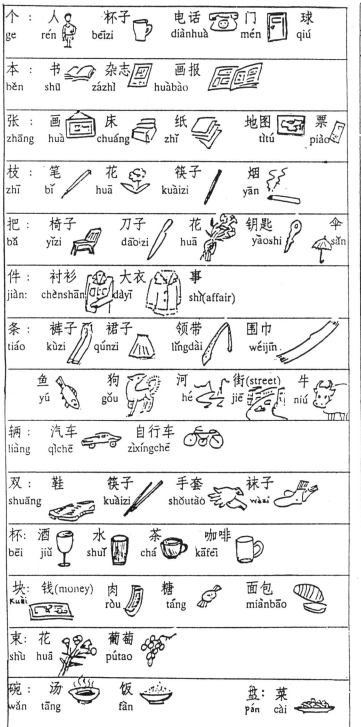

| 个 : 人 rén | 杯子 bēizi | 电话 diànhuà | 门 mén | 球 qiú |
| ge | | | | |

| 门 : 课 (course) kè | 节 :(session of class) 课 jié |
| mén | |

| 本 : 书 shū | 杂志 zázhì | 画报 huàbào |
| běn | | |

| 套 : 书 shū | 沙发 (sofa) shāfā | 衣服 yīfu |
| tào | | |

| 张 : 画 huà | 床 chuáng | 纸 zhǐ | 地图 dìtú | 票 piào |
| zhāng | | | | |

| 付 : 眼镜 yǎnjìng | 手套 shǒutào |
| fù | |

| 枝 : 笔 bǐ | 花 huā | 筷子 kuàizi | 烟 yān |
| zhī | | | |

| 瓶: 酒 jiǔ | 可口可乐 kěkǒukělè | 牛奶 niúnǎi |
| píng | | |

| 把 : 椅子 yǐzi | 刀子 dāozi | 花 huā | 钥匙 yàoshi | 伞 sǎn |
| bǎ | | | | |

| 封 : 信 xìn | 位 : 客人 kèrén |
| fēng | wèi |

| 件 : 衬衫 chènshān | 大衣 dàyī | 事 shì(affair) |
| jiàn: | | |

| 种 (kind): 书 shū | 花 huā | 东西 dōngxi |
| zhǒng | | |

| 条 : 裤子 kùzi | 裙子 qúnzi | 领带 lǐngdài | 围巾 wéijīn |
| tiáo | | | |

| 只 : 猫 māo | 老鼠 lǎoshǔ |
| zhī | |

| 鱼 yú | 狗 gǒu | 河 hé | 街 (street) jiē | 牛 niú |

| 片 (slice): 面包 miànbāo | 肉 ròu |
| piàn | |

| 辆 : 汽车 qìchē | 自行车 zìxíngchē |
| liàng | |

| 架 : 飞机 fēijī | 电视机 diànshìjī | 收音机 shōuyīnjī |
| jià | | |

| 双 : 鞋 | 筷子 kuàizi | 手套 shǒutào | 袜子 wàzi |
| shuāng | | | |

| 棵 : 树 shù | 菜 cài |
| kē | |

| 杯: 酒 jiǔ | 水 shuǐ | 茶 chá | 咖啡 kāfēi |
| bēi | | | |

| 根 : 烟 yān | 针 zhēn | 头发 tóufa |
| gēn | | |

| 块 : 钱 (money) | 肉 ròu | 糖 táng | 面包 miànbāo |
| Kuài | | | |

| 间 : 房间 fángjiān |
| jiān | |

| 束 : 花 huā | 葡萄 pútao |
| shù | |

| 座 : 楼 lóu | 山 shān | 桥 qiáo | 庙 (temple) miào |
| zuò | | | |

| 碗 : 汤 tāng | 饭 fàn | 盘: 菜 cài |
| wǎn | | pán |

# 部首表　THE 189 RADICALS

| RADICAL, MEANING | ANCIENT FORM | COMMON POSITIONS | EXAMPLES (from the text) | RADICAL, MEANING | ANCIENT FORM | COMMON POSITIONS | EXAMPLES (from the text) |
|---|---|---|---|---|---|---|---|
| 丶 | | | 主桌半为(為) | 阝(在右) city | | | 都那部 |
| 一 one | 一 | | 三下才七上 | 凵 receptacle | | | 凶画 |
| 丨 | | | 中半书(書)旧(舊) | 力 strength | | | 助动加劳努务办 |
| 丿 | | | 么生用反每右 | 氵 water | | | 法河注汉滑游泳 |
| 乙(一乛乚) | | | 九也买习电民 | 忄(小) heart | | | 快忙怕情惯慢懂 |
| 亠 cover | | | 六产高京齐就 | 宀 roof | | | 宇家完安室宿容 |
| 冫 ice | | | 冬尽冷决冰冻 | 广 broad | | | 应床店庆 |
| 冖 to cover | | | 写军农(農) | 门(門) door | | | 间开关问 |
| 讠(言) word | | | 请说词认(認)识(識) | 辶(辶) walk | | | 边达过还送遇遍 |
| 二 two | 二 | | 五互开专无干些 | 寸 inch | | | 导专(专)对(對) |
| 十 ten | 十 | | 千午华南卖真(眞) | 扌 hand | | | 找报握操打 |
| 厂 cliff, plant | | | 历原厚压殿(厂) | 工 work | | | 左差 |
| 匚 basket | | | 医区巨 | 土 earth | | | 地块场坐址堂在 |
| 卜(卜) to divine | | | 处卦占 | 士 scholar | | | 声喜 |
| 刂 knife | | | 别刮到刻判利前 | 艹 grass | | | 花茶英菜黄薄蓝葡萄 |
| 冂 borders | | | 同再 | 大 big | | | 头买太天 |
| 八(丷) eight | 八 | | 分公关首共兴 | 廾(在下) folded hands | | | 开异 |
| 人(入) man | | | 个今介会舍从来 | 尢 crooked | | | 就龙尤 |
| 亻 man | | | 你们他体但健休 | 弋 a dart | | | 式 |
| 勹 wrap | | | 句包够 | 小(⺌) small | | | 少光当党堂常 |
| 刀(⺈) knife | | | 负争 切 | 口 mouth | | | 叫吗吃唸号品吸告 |
| 几(凡) table | | | 风凡 | 囗 enclosure | | | 国(國)图(圖)园(園)回 |
| 儿 man | | | 先克光党 | 巾 kerchief | | | 师帮市常布帽 |
| 厶 private | | | 去县参能 | 山 mountain | | | 岁(歲)崎岖 |
| 又(又) also | | | 友反发对难欢 | 彳 step | | | 行待很後(后)從(从) |
| 辶 walk | | | 迫迁建 | 彡 long hairs | | | 须影 |

| Radical | Examples | Radical | Examples |
|---|---|---|---|
| 卩 seal | 即却卫 | 夕 evening | 外多夜名岁 |
| 阝(在左) mound | 阳阶际院险 | 夂 from back | 冬条夏复 |
| 犭 animal | 狗猪狮 | 瓦 tile | 瓶瓩瓷 |
| 𠆢(食) eat | 饭(飯)馆(館) | 止 stop | 正整歷(历) |
| 彐(彑彐) pig | 当(當) | 攴 rap | 敲敛 |
| 尸 corpse | 展屋尾 | 日 sun | 早易星明时春者 |
| 己(巳) self | 导 | 曰(日) say | 會(会)書(书)最 |
| 弓 a bow | 张强 | 水(氵) water | 泉永 |
| 子(孑) child | 学孔 | 贝(貝) cowry | 责贵买(买)卖(卖) |
| 屮 sprout | 芻屯 | 见(兒) see | 观觉览 |
| 女 female | 她好妈妈姓要 | 父 father | 爷爸 |
| 幺 small | 乡幾(几)樂(乐) | 牛(牜) cattle | 特牺牲牧牛 |
| 纟(糸) silk | 红纸织经结给绩 | 手 hand | 拿掌拳 |
| 马(馬) horse | 骂验 | 毛 hair | 毫毡 |
| 巛 | 灾巢 | 气 air | 氧氢气(氣) |
| 灬 fire | 点(點)热(熱)照 | 攵 literary | 教放故敲敝 |
| 斗 peck | 斜料 | 片 a strip | 版牌 |
| 文 literary | 齐吝 | 斤 axe | 新所断欣 |
| 方 square | 放旅旗旁 | 爪(爫) claws | 受爱(愛)爬 |
| 火 fire | 灯(燈)烟(煙) | 月(肉) moon | 朋服脸背能期望 |
| 心 heart | 忘志念想思意您 | 欠 owe | 欢次歌欧 |
| 户 door | 所房雇 | 风(風) wind | 飚飘 |
| 礻(示) reveal | 礼社视 | 殳 lance | 杀毁段 |
| 王 king, jade | 玩现班理望球 | 聿(聿書) stylus | 書(书)肃 |
| 韦(韋) leather | 韧韩 | 爿 slice | 牀(床)将 |
| 木 tree | 东(東)椅枝相树本 | 毋(母) do not / mother | 每毒 |
| 犬 dog | 状哭 | 穴 cave | 穷究空穿 |
| 歹 bad | 死残殃 | 立 to stand | 意竟 站端 |

| Radical | Early form | Seal/Bronze | Derived characters | Radical | Early form | Seal/Bronze | Derived characters |
|---|---|---|---|---|---|---|---|
| 瓜 melon | 瓜 | 瓜 | 瓢瓤 | 赤 red | 赤 | 赤 | 赧糖赫 |
| 鸟(鳥) bird | 鸣鸟 | 鸣鸟 | 鸡鸭鹅鸳 | 豆 bean | 豆豆 | 豆豐 | 头(头)登豈豐(丰) |
| 用 use | 甬 | 甬 | 甬甭 | 酉 spirits | 酉 | 酉 | 配酤醒酪 |
| 矛 lance | 矛矛 | 矛矛 | 柔务(矜) | 辰 hour | 辰 | 辰 | 辱農(农) |
| 疋(正) cloth | 疋 | 疋足 | 蛋楚疑 | 豕 pig | 豕 | 豕豕 | 豬象 |
| 皮 skin | 皮 | 皮皮 | 颇皱 | 卤(鹵) brine | 卤卤 | 卤 | 咸 |
| 衣 clothes | 衣 | 衣 | 袋装裹表 | 里 hamlet | 里 | 里重 | 野重 |
| 羊(芊羊) sheep | 芊羊 | 羔羊 | 羌着美 | 足(疋) foot | 足足 | 足 | 跟跃践跑跳路 |
| 米 rice | 米米 | 米 | 粉糖料精 | 豸 reptile | 豸 | 豸 | 貓貌豹 |
| 来 plough | 来 | 耒 | 耕 | 谷 valley | 谷谷 | 谷 | 欲卻 |
| 老 old | 老老 | 者 | 者考者 | 采 distinguish | | 采番 | 释番 |
| 耳 ear | 耳 | 取耳 | 取耻联聪聰聋 | 身 body | 身 | 身 | 躲躯射 |
| 臣 minister | 臣 | 臣臣 | 卧临 | 角 horn | 角角 | 角 | 解触 |
| 西(襾) | 西西 | 西 | 要票 | 辛 bitter | 辛 | 辛辛 | 辨辩辞 |
| 页(頁) head | 页 | 顶 | 预须头领题 | 青 blue | 青 | 青睛 | 静靖 |
| 车(車) vehicle | 車車 | 轩 | 轻转轧 | 疒 sickness | 疒 | 疒 | 病疼疾疲 |
| 比 compare | 比 | 皆 | 毕皆 | 衤 clothes | 衣 | 衤 | 初被袍 |
| 戈 spear | 戈 | 戈划 | 成我或战划 | 示 reveal | 示 | 示 | 票禁 |
| 石 stone | 石 | 矿石 | 确破研硬碰磨 | 艮(艮) perverse | 艮艮 | 艮艮 | 艰既 |
| 龙(龍) dragon | 龙 | 龙 | 聋垄 | 竹(𥫗) bamboo | 竹竹 | 竹 | 笔第笑笨简算節节 |
| 业 | | 业 | 业(业)丛 | 臼 mortar | 臼臼 | 臼臼 | 兜舊(旧) |
| 目 eye | 目目 | 冒眀 | 看省睡眼眶 | 自 self | 自 | 自 | 息臭 |
| 田 land | 田 | 冒冒 | 男累备留畜 | 血 blood | 血血 | 血 | 衆 |
| 网 net | 网 | 网 | 罗罪 | 舟 boat | 舟舟 | 舟 | 船航 |
| 皿 dish | 皿皿 | 皿 | 益盗盟 | 羽 feather | 羽羽 | 羽 | 習(习) |
| 钅(金) gold | 金 | 钅 | 钢铅钟钱错 | 糸 silk | 糸 | 糸 | 紧素系 |
| 矢 arrow | 矢 | 知 | 知短 | 言 word | 言言 | 言 | 誉警誓 |
| 禾 grain | 禾禾 | 禾禾 | 和私秋科种香 | 麦(麥) wheat | 麦麦 | 麦 | 麯 |
| 白 white | 白 | 白皂的 | 百皂的 | 走 walk | 走走 | 走 | 起赴赶超 |

| | | | | | | | |
|---|---|---|---|---|---|---|---|
| 虍 tiger | 虍 | 虎 虎 | 處(处) 號(号) | * 其 its (lit) | 其 | 甚 其 | 基 期 欺 |
| * 虫 insect | 虫 | 虫 | 蚊 蛇 | * 雨(雷) rain | 雨 | 雪 | 雷 電(电) 雪 需 |
| * 缶 clay pot | 缶 | 缶 | 缺 缸 | * 齿(齒) tooth | 齒 | 齿 | 龄 |
| * 舌 tongue | 舌 | 舌 | 甜 乱 辞 舘 | * 黾(黽) toad | 黽 | 黽 | 鼋 |
| * 金 metal | 金 | 金 | 鉴 | * 門 fight | 鬥 | 鬥 | 鬧 鬩 鬮 |
| * 隹 bird | 隹 | 隹 隹 | 隻 售 集 难 雖 雜(杂) | 髟 hair | 髟 | 髟 | 髮 鬚 |
| * 鱼(魚) fish | 魚 | 鱼 魚 | 鲜 鯉 魯 | * 麻 hemp | 麻 | 麻 | 磨 麼(么) |
| * 音 sound | 音 | 音 音 | 韵 響 | * 鹿 deer | 鹿 | 鹿 鹿 | 塵(尘) 麒 麟 |
| * 革 rawhide | 革 | 革 革 | 鞋 鞏 | * 黑 black | 黑 | 黑 黑 | 點(点) 默 黨(党) |
| * 骨 bone | 骨 | 骨 | 體(体) | * 鼠 rat | 鼠 | 鼠 | 鼬 |
| * 食 eat | 食 | 食 食 | 湌 餐 | * 鼻 nose | 鼻 | 鼻 | 鼾 |
| * 鬼 ghost | 鬼 | 鬼 鬼 鬼 | 魁 魔 魂 | | | | |

This radical chart is based on 新华字典.  One character
sometimes appears in more than one radical, not necessarily
related to its meaning.

* indicates this radical is also a character.

汉语课本
（第一、二册）

# VOCABULARY LIST
## (ENGLISH TO CHINESE)

| English | 汉字 | Pinyin | Lesson |
|---|---|---|---|
| able | 能 | néng | 26 |
| abundant | 丰富 豐富 | fēngfù | 47 |
| accustomed to | 习惯 習慣 | xíguàn | 33 |
| ache | 疼 | téng | 46 |
| achievement | 成绩 | chéngjī | 35 |
| actor | 演员 | yǎnyuán | 49 |
| address | 地址 | dìzhǐ | 20 |
| advance | 进步 進步 | jìnbù | 29 |
| adviser | 顾问 顧問 | gùwèn | 42 |
| afraid | 怕 | pà | 33 |
| Africa | 非洲 | Fēizhōu | 45 |
| afternoon | 下午 | xiàwǔ | 18 |
| afterwards | 后来 後來 | hòulái | 45 |
| again | 又 | yòu | 27 |
| age | 岁数 歲數 | suìshu | 42 |
| aged | 老 | lǎo | 31 |
| airmail (letter) | 航空(信) | hángkōng (xìn) | 34 |
| airplane | 飞机 飛機 | fēijī | 29 |
| airport | 机场 機場 | jīchǎng | 29 |
| all | 都 | dōu | 3 |
| alley | 胡同 | hútòng | 38 |
| almond | 杏仁 | xìngrén | 43 |
| almond junket | 杏仁豆腐 | xìngréndòufu | 43 |
| already | 已经 已經 | yǐjīng | 31 |
| also | 也 | yě | 2 |
| although | 虽然 雖然 | suīrán | 39 |
| altogether | 一共 | yīgòng | 36 |
| always | 总 總 | zǒng | 22 |
| always, forever | 永远 永遠 | yǒngyuǎn | 39 |
| ambassador | 大使 | dàshǐ | 27 |
| ancient | 古 | gǔ | 33 |

| English | 汉字 | Pinyin | Lesson |
|---|---|---|---|
| and, with | 和 | hé | 13 |
| anger someone (v.) | 气人 氣人 | qìrén | 28 |
| animal | 动物 動物 | dòngwu | 45 |
| anniversary | 周年 週年 | zhōunián | 50 |
| another | 别的 | biéde | 43 |
| answer | 回答 | huídá | 24 |
| answer (the phone) | 接(电话)(電話) | jiē (diànhuà) | 23 |
| anxious, nervous (to feel ~) | 着急 | zháo jí | 35 |
| applaud (v.) | 鼓掌 | gǔ zhǎng | 40 |
| apple | 苹果 | píngguǒ | 19 |
| appointment | 约会 約會 | yuēhuì | 47 |
| arrange, put in order | 整理 | zhénglǐ | 22 |
| arrest, catch (v.) | 抓 | zhuā | 49 |
| arrive at (v.) | 到 | dào | 27 |
| art | 艺术 藝術 | yìshù | 42 |
| art exhibition | 画展 畫展 | huàzhǎn | 50 |
| artist | 艺术家 藝術家 | yìshùjiā | 49 |
| ask (v.) | 问 問 | wèn | 9 |
| assembly hall | 礼堂 禮堂 | lǐtáng | 42 |
| at | 在 | zài | 10 |
| at ease | 放心 | fàngxīn | 29 |
| at once | 就 | jiù | 26 |
| athlete | 运动员 運動員 | yùndòngyuán | 40 |
| attend (meeting) | 开会 開會 | kāi huì | 31 |
| attend (a class) | 上(课)(課) | shàng (kè) | 17 |
| attend (v.) | 参加 參加 | cānjiā | 20 |
| attend to (v.) | 办 辦 | bàn | 28 |
| attendant | 服务员 服務員 | fúwùyuán | 19 |
| attract (v.) | 吸引 | xīyǐn | 49 |
| audience | 观众 觀眾 | guānzhòng | 40 |
| auditorium | 礼堂 禮堂 | lǐtáng | 42 |

| English | 汉字 | Pinyin | Lesson |
|---|---|---|---|
| brandy | 白兰地 白蘭地 | báilándì | 27 |
| bread | 面包 麵包 | miànbāo | 25 |
| break | 打破 | dǎpò | 40 |
| break (from work) | 休息 | xiūxi | 18 |
| breakfast | 早饭 早飯 | zǎofàn | 28 |
| bridge | 桥 橋 | qiáo | 44 |
| bright | 聪明 聰明 | cōngming | 39 |
| bright | 晴 | qíng | 33 |
| bright, light | 亮 | liàng | 43 |
| bring (v.) | 带 帶 | dài | 38 |
| bring up | 培养 培養 | péiyǎng | 47 |
| Britain | 英国 英國 | Yīngguó | 13 |
| broadcast (v.) | 广播 廣播 | guǎngbō | 40 |
| broadcasting room | 广播室 廣播室 | guǎngbōshì | 41 |
| brother (older) | 哥哥 | gēge | 3 |
| build | 个子 個子 | gèzi | 32 |
| build (v.) | 建设 建設 | jiànshè | 31 |
| build (v.) | 建筑 建筑 | jiànzhù | 41 |
| build, repair (v.) | 修 | xiū | 42 |
| building | 建筑 建築 | jiànzhù | 41 |
| building; floor | 楼 樓 | lóu | 27 |
| bunch | 束 | shù | 21 |
| bus | 公共汽车 公共汽車 | gōnggòng qìchē | 38 |
| business | 事(儿)(兒) | shì(r) | 17 |
| business trip | 出差 | chū chāi | 44 |
| busy | 忙 | máng | 3 |
| but | 但是 | dànshì | 39 |
| but | 可是 | kěshì | 26 |
| buy (v.) | 买 買 | mǎi | 13 |
| cable | 电报 電報 | diànbao | 34 |
| call (a name) (v.) | 叫 | jiào | 9 |
| call for (a cab) | 叫 | jiào | 29 |

| English | 汉字 | Pinyin | Lesson |
|---|---|---|---|
| call on | 找 | zhǎo | 16 |
| camera | 照相机 照相機 | zhàoxiàngjī | 41 |
| camera lens | 镜头 鏡頭 | jìngtóu | 42 |
| can (v.) | 了 | liǎo | 42 |
| can, able (v.) | 能 | néng | 26 |
| can, know how (v.) | 会 會 | huì | 26 |
| cap | 帽子 | màozi | 28 |
| capital | 首都 | shǒudū | 31 |
| car, vehicle | 车 車 | chē | 5 |
| care | 关心 關心 | guānxīn | 39 |
| careful | 当心 當心 | dāngxīn | 43 |
| catch a cold (v.) | 感冒 | gǎnmào | 46 |
| cattle | 牛 | niú | 47 |
| center | 中间 中間 | zhōngjiān | 22 |
| centimeter | 公分 | gōngfēn | 37 |
| central unit | 总机 總機 | zǒngjī | 23 |
| certainly | 一定 | yídìng | 20 |
| certificate of merit | 奖状 獎狀 | jiǎngzhuàng | 42 |
| chair | 椅子 | yǐzi | 22 |
| chairman | 主席 | zhǔxí | 40 |
| champagne | 香槟酒 香檳酒 | xiāngbīnjiǔ | 27 |
| chance, opportunity | 机会 機會 | jīhuì | 35 |
| change (small cash) | 零钱 零錢 | língqián | 36 |
| change (v.) | 换 換 | huàn | 38 |
| character, figure | 人物 | rénwù | 44 |
| character, word | 字 | zì | 15 |
| chart | 图片 圖片 | túpiàn | 34 |
| chauffer | 司机 司機 | sījī | 41 |
| cheap | 便宜 | piányi | 36 |
| check-up | 检查 檢查 | jiǎnchá | 32 |
| cheese | 奶酪 | nǎilào | 25 |

| English | 汉字 | | Pinyin | Lesson |
|---|---|---|---|---|
| construct, construction | 建筑 | 建筑 | jiànzhù | 41 |
| construction site | 工地 | | gōngdì | 42 |
| convenient | 方便 | | fāngbiàn | 42 |
| cooked rice | 饭 | 飯 | fàn | 18 |
| cool | 凉快 | | liángkuài | 33 |
| copy (of a painting, etc.) | 临摹 | 臨摹 | línmó | 50 |
| cordial | 亲切 | 親切 | qīnqiè | 43 |
| cordial | 热情 | 熱情 | rèqíng | 30 |
| correct | 对 | 對 | duì | 13 |
| correct | 正确 | 正確 | zhèngquè | 49 |
| correct (adj) | 不错 | 不錯 | bùcuò | 25 |
| correct (v.) | 改 | | gǎi | 47 |
| cotton cloth | 布 | | bù | 37 |
| cough (v.) | 咳嗽 | | késou | 46 |
| counselor | 参赞 | 參贊 | cānzàn | 27 |
| counter | 柜台 | 櫃台 | guìtái | 34 |
| country | 国 | 國 | guó | 6 |
| countryside | 农村 | 農村 | nóngcūn | 24 |
| courtyard | 院子 | | yuànzi | 47 |
| cover | 盖儿 | 蓋兒 | gàir | 47 |
| cover | 面儿 | 面兒 | miànr | 37 |
| criticism | 意见 | | yìjiàn | 43 |
| cross over/through (v.) | 穿 | | chuān | 43 |
| crossing | 路口 | | lùkǒu | 38 |
| crowded, squeeze (v.) | 挤 | 擠 | jǐ | 41 |
| cry | 哭 | | kū | 30 |
| culture | 文化 | | wénhuà | 27 |
| custom | 风俗 | 風俗 | fēngsú | 48 |
| customer | 顾客 | 顧客 | gùkè | 43 |
| cute, lovely | 可爱 | 可愛 | kě'ài | 45 |

| English | 汉字 | | Pinyin | Lesson |
|---|---|---|---|---|
| cymbidium (orchid) | 兰花 | 蘭花 | lánhuā | 50 |
| dance | 舞蹈 | | wǔdǎo | 49 |
| dance | 舞会 | 舞會 | wǔhuì | 20 |
| dance (v.) | 跳舞 | | tiàowǔ | 21 |
| dark | 黑暗 | | hēi'àn | 49 |
| date | 日 | | rì | 20 |
| date tree | 枣树 | 棗樹 | zǎoshù | 47 |
| day | 天 | | tiān | 18 |
| dear | 亲爱的 | 親愛的 | qīn'àide | 48 |
| decide (v.) | 决定 | | juédìng | 44 |
| deepen | 加深 | | jiāshēn | 26 |
| delegate | 代表 | | dàibiǎo | 23 |
| delegation | 代表团 | 代表團 | dàibiǎotuán | 23 |
| delicious | 好吃 | | hǎochī | 21 |
| department | 系 | | xì | 15 |
| department, section | 科 | | kē | 46 |
| design (v.) | 设计 | 設計 | shèjì | 47 |
| develop | 发展 | 發展 | fāzhǎn | 36 |
| develop (a film) | 洗 | | xǐ | 42 |
| dialled the wrong number | 打错了 | 打錯了 | dǎ cuò le | 23 |
| diary | 日记 | 日記 | rìjì | 9 |
| dictionary | 词典 | 詞典 | cídiǎn | 11 |
| die | 死 | | sǐ | 41 |
| difficult | 难 | 難 | nán | 24 |
| difficult, hard | 辛苦 | | xīnkǔ | 31 |
| dimsum | 点心 | 點心 | diǎnxīn | 24 |
| dining hall | 食堂 | | shítáng | 17 |
| dining room | 餐厅 | 餐廳 | cāntīng | 22 |
| direction | 方向 | | fāngxiàng | 38 |
| director | 经理 | 經理 | jīnglǐ | 14 |
| director | 主任 | | zhǔrèn | 39 |

| English | 汉字 | 汉字 | Pinyin | Lesson |
|---|---|---|---|---|
| disappeared | 绝 | 絕 | jué | 33 |
| dish | 菜 | | cài | 27 |
| distant place | 远方 | 遠方 | yuǎnfāng | 39 |
| do | 作 | | zuò | 14 |
| do (shadowboxing) | 打 | | dǎ | 40 |
| do business | 营业 | 營業 | yíngyè | 34 |
| do, handle, attend to, tackle | 办 | 辦 | bàn | 28 |
| doctor | 大夫 | | dàifu | 5 |
| doesn't matter | 没关系 | 沒關係 | méi guānxi | 41 |
| don't (v.) | 别 | | bié | 19 |
| door | 门 | 門 | mén | 21 |
| doorway, entrance | 门口 | 門口 | ménkǒu | 41 |
| dormitory | 宿舍 | | sùshè | 10 |
| drama (spoken) | 话剧 | 話劇 | huàjù | 49 |
| draw, paint (v.) | 画 | 畫 | huà | 36 |
| drawing room | 客厅 | 客廳 | kètīng | 22 |
| drink (v.) | 喝 | | hē | 8 |
| drive (a car) (v.) | 开(车) | 開(車) | kāi (chē) | 23 |
| driver | 司机 | 司機 | sījī | 41 |
| dumpling | 饺子 | 餃子 | jiǎozi | 46 |
| each other | 互相 | | hùxiāng | 15 |
| each, every | 每 | | měi | 18 |
| each, every: various | 各 | | gè | 43 |
| ear | 耳朵 | | ěrduo | 32 |
| early | 早 | | zǎo | 26 |
| earn, make money | 挣 | | zhèng | 35 |
| east | 东(边) | 東(邊) | dōng (biān) | 38 |
| eat | 吃 | | chī | 18 |
| eight | 八 | | bā | 11 |
| election | 选举 | 選舉 | xuǎnjǔ | 39 |
| elephant | 象 | | xiàng | 45 |

| English | 汉字 | 汉字 | Pinyin | Lesson |
|---|---|---|---|---|
| else, in addition to | 还 | 還 | hái | 15 |
| embarrassed | 不好意思 | | bù hǎoyìsi | 39 |
| embassy | 大使馆 | 大使館 | dàshǐguǎn | 27 |
| emissary | 使者 | | shǐzhě | 45 |
| emperor | 皇帝 | | huángdì | 41 |
| engaged (phone) | 占线 | 占線 | zhànxiàn | 23 |
| engineer | 工程师 | 工程師 | gōngchéngshī | 14 |
| English | 英语 | 英語 | yīngyǔ | 12 |
| enough, sufficient | 够 | 夠 | gòu | 43 |
| enter (v.) | 进来 | 進來 | jìn lái | 26 |
| enter, come in (v.) | 进 | 進 | jìn | 8 |
| enthusiastic, cordial | 热情 | 熱情 | rèqíng | 30 |
| enthusiastic, warm | 热烈 | 熱烈 | rèliè | 40 |
| entire | 全 | | quán | 48 |
| entrance, doorway | 门口 | 門口 | ménkǒu | 41 |
| envelope | 信封 | | xìnfēng | 34 |
| envoy | 使者 | | shǐzhě | 45 |
| erect | 立 | | lì | 33 |
| error | 错误 | 錯誤 | cuòwù | 47 |
| Europe | 欧洲 | 歐洲 | Ōu Zhōu | 7 |
| even | 连...也... | 連...也... | lián...yě... | 49 |
| even/still more | 更 | | gèng | 21 |
| evening | 晚上 | | wǎnshang | 16 |
| every, each | 每 | | měi | 18 |
| every, various | 各 | | gè | 43 |
| examination | 考试 | 考試 | kǎoshì | 35 |
| examine (v.) | 考 | | kǎo | 35 |
| examine (x-ray) | 透视 | 透視 | tòushì | 32 |
| excited | 激动 | 激動 | jīdòng | 40 |
| excrement | 大便 | | dàbiàn | 46 |
| exercise (physical) | 运动 | 運動 | yùndòng | 28.40 |
| exercise (physical) | 锻炼 | 鍛煉 | duànliàn | 24 |

| English | 汉字 | 汉字 | Pinyin | Lesson |
|---|---|---|---|---|
| exercise (written) | 练习 | 練習 | liànxí | 24 |
| exhausting | 辛苦 | | xīnkǔ | 31 |
| expensive | 贵 | | guì | 36 |
| explain (v.) | 讲解 | 講解 | jiǎngjiě | 47 |
| extend; connect | 接 | | jiē | 47 |
| extension (phone) | 分机 | 分機 | fēnjī | 23 |
| extremely | 非常 | | fēicháng | 21 |
| extremely | …极了 | …極了 | jíle | 40 |
| eye | 眼睛 | | yǎnjing | 32 |
| fabric | 料子 | | liàozi | 37 |
| factory | 工厂 | 工廠 | gōngchǎng | 23 |
| fair, unbiased | 公平 | | gōngpíng | 28 |
| fall ill (v.) | 得病 | | débìng | 32 |
| familiar with | 认识 | 認識 | rènshi | 12 |
| family | 家 | | jiā | 14 |
| famous | 有名 | | yǒumíng | 23 |
| far | 远 | 遠 | yuǎn | 30 |
| fast, quick | 快 | | kuài | 25 |
| fat, loose-fitting | 肥 | | féi | 37 |
| fat, stout | 胖 | | pàng | 37 |
| father | 爸爸 | | bàba | 4 |
| fear; afraid | 怕 | | pà | 33 |
| feces | 大便 | | dàbiàn | 46 |
| feel | 觉得 | 覺得 | juéde | 33 |
| feel anxious | 着急 | | zháojí | 35 |
| feeling | 感想 | | gǎnxiǎng | 47 |
| female | 女 | | nǚ | 12 |
| festival | 节 | 節 | jié | 48 |
| fever | 发烧 | 發燒 | fāshāo | 46 |
| few | 少 | | shǎo | 22 |
| figure, character | 人物 | | rénwù | 44 |

| English | 汉字 | 汉字 | Pinyin | Lesson |
|---|---|---|---|---|
| full (v.) | 填 | | tián | 32 |
| film | 电影 | 電影 | diànyǐng | 17 |
| fine (weather), bright/clear (day) | 晴 | | qíng | 33 |
| finish | 了 | | liǎo | 42 |
| finish (v.) | 完 | | wán | 39 |
| firecracker | 爆竹 | | bàozhú | 48 |
| first | 先 | | xiān | 32 |
| first secretary | 一秘 | | yīmì | 27 |
| fish | 鱼 | 魚 | yú | 25 |
| fish (v.) | 钓 | 釣 | diào | 25 |
| five | 五 | | wǔ | 10 |
| flag, banner | 旗子 | | qízi | 40 |
| flavor, style | 风味 | 風味 | fēngwèi | 43 |
| floor; building | 楼 | 樓 | lóu | 27 |
| flower | 花儿 | 花兒 | huār | 21 |
| fluent | 流利 | | liúlì | 25 |
| fluoroscope, X-ray machine | 透视 | | tòushì | 32 |
| fog | 雾 | 霧 | wù | 33 |
| folk music | 民乐 | 民樂 | mínyuè | 49 |
| folk song | 民歌 | | míngē | 19 |
| follow | 跟 | | gēn | 17 |
| fond of | 喜欢 | 喜歡 | xǐhuān | 19 |
| food | 饭 | 飯 | fàn | 18 |
| foot | 脚 | | jiǎo | 41 |
| for (the sake of) | 为 | 為 | wèi | 27 |
| for (toward) | 对 | 對 | duì | 39 |
| force, compel (v.) | 逼 | | bī | 49 |
| forecast | 预报 | 預報 | yùbào | 33 |
| foreign country | 外国 | 外國 | wàiguó | 45 |
| foreign language | 外语 | 外語 | wàiyǔ | 9 |
| foreign student | 留学生 | 留學生 | liúxuéshēng | 9 |

| English | 汉字 | Pinyin | Lesson |
|---|---|---|---|
| green tea | 绿茶 | lǜchá | 19 |
| grow, plant (v.) | 种 | zhǒng | 46 |
| gruel | 粥 | zhōu | 43 |
| guest | 客人 | kèren | 39 |
| guide | 向导 | xiàngdǎo | 41 |
| guide (by speech) | 讲解员 | jiǎngjiěyuán | 47 |
| hair | 头发 | tóufa | 32 |
| ham | 火腿 | huǒtuǐ | 25 |
| hand | 手 | shǒu | 46 |
| handle (v.) | 办 | bàn | 28 |
| hang (v.) | 吊 | diào | 41 |
| hang, put up (v.) | 挂 | guà | 34 |
| Happy New Year | 恭贺新禧 | gōnghèxīnxǐ | 48 |
| happy | 愉快 | yúkuài | 39 |
| happy, glad | 高兴 | gāoxìng | 21 |
| hard, difficult | 辛苦 | xīnkǔ | 31 |
| hard-working, studious | 努力 | nǔlì | 29 |
| hare | 兔子 | tùzi | 48 |
| hat, cap | 帽子 | màozi | 28 |
| have | 有 | yǒu | 14 |
| he | 他 | tā | 3 |
| head | 头 | tóu | 45 |
| health | 健康 | jiànkāng | 27 |
| heart | 心 | xīn | 30 |
| heart (organ) | 心脏 | xīnzàng | 32 |
| heavy | 重 | zhòng | 42 |
| height, stature | 个子 | gèzi | 32 |
| hello | 喂 | wèi | 13 |
| help (v. or n.) | 帮助 | bāngzhù | 22 |
| help (v.) | 帮 | bāng | 22 |
| hen's egg | 鸡蛋 | jīdàn | 25 |

| English | 汉字 | Pinyin | Lesson |
|---|---|---|---|
| here | 这儿 | zhèr | 16 |
| heritage | 遗产 | yíchǎn | 47 |
| hill | 山 | shān | 41 |
| hire; call for (a cab. etc.) | 叫 | jiào | 29 |
| history | 历史 | lìshǐ | 36 |
| holiday | 节日 | jiérì | 48 |
| holiday (to have) | 放假 | fàngjià | 35 |
| hope | 希望 | xīwàng | 31 |
| horse | 马 | mǎ | 38 |
| hospital | 医院 | yīyuàn | 46 |
| hospital ward | 病房 | bìngfáng | 46 |
| hospitalized | 住院 | zhùyuàn | 46 |
| hot | 热 | rè | 33 |
| hotel | 旅馆 | lǚguǎn | 41 |
| hour | 小时 | xiǎoshí | 31 |
| house | 房子 | fángzi | 22 |
| how | 多 | duō | 44 |
| how is that? | 怎么样 | zěnmeyàng | 22 |
| how many | 几 | jǐ | 15 |
| how much | 多少 | duōshao | 10 |
| how, very | 多么 | duōme | 44 |
| how, why | 怎么 | zěnme | 38 |
| how?; how is that? | 怎么样 | zěnmeyàng | 22 |
| hundred | 百 | bǎi | 33 |
| hungry | 饿 | è | 43 |
| husband | 爱人 | àiren | 14 |
| I | 我 | wǒ | 2 |
| ice skate (v.) | 滑冰 | huá bīng | 28 |
| ice skates | 冰鞋 | bīngxié | 28 |
| ideal | 理想 | lǐxiǎng | 26 |
| if | 要是 | yàoshi | 41 |

| English | 汉字 | Pinyin | Lesson |
|---|---|---|---|
| ill; illness | 病 | bìng | 32 |
| immediately | 立刻 | lìkè | 46 |
| immediately, at once | 就 | jiù | 26 |
| impartial, fair | 公平 | gōngpíng | 28 |
| Imperial Palace | 故官 | Gùgōng | 41 |
| impression, feeling | 感想 | gǎnxiǎng | 47 |
| improve | 提高 | tígāo | 36 |
| in addition to, else | 还 還 | hái | 15 |
| in earnest | 认真 認真 | rènzhēn | 24 |
| in, at | 在 | zài | 10 |
| increase (v.) | 提高 | tígāo | 36 |
| inexpensive | 便宜 | piányi | 36 |
| injection; needle | 针 | zhēn | 46 |
| inside | 里边 裡邊 | lǐbiān | 22 |
| intelligent, bright | 聪明 聰明 | cōngmíng | 39 |
| interesting | 有意思 | yǒu yìsi | 20 |
| international | 国际 國際 | guójì | 31 |
| internal medicine | 内科 | nèikē | 32 |
| interpreter | 翻译 翻譯 | fānyì | 26 |
| interview (v.) | 访问 訪問 | fǎngwèn | 23 |
| introduce | 介绍 | jièshào | 13 |
| it | 它 | tā | 44 |
| item | 节目 節目 | jiémù | 49 |
| jacket | 上衣 | shàngyī | 16 |
| jacket (padded) | 棉袄 棉襖 | mián'ǎo | 37 |
| jade | 玉 | yù | 36 |
| Japan | 日本 | Rìběn | 21 |
| job | 活儿 活兒 | huór | 42 |
| jujube | 枣树 棗樹 | zǎoshù | 47 |
| jump (v.) | 跳 | tiào | 44 |
| just (adv.) | 刚 剛 | gāng | 38 |

| English | 汉字 | Pinyin | Lesson |
|---|---|---|---|
| keep, to retain (v.) | 保持 | bǎochí | 40 |
| kick (v.) | 踢 | tī | 28 |
| kill (v.) | 杀 殺 | shā | 49 |
| kilogram | 公斤 | gōngjīn | 42 |
| kind, type (measure) | 种 種 | zhǒng | 36 |
| kitchen | 厨房 | chúfáng | 22 |
| knock (v.) | 敲 | qiāo | 33 |
| know (a fact) (v.) | 知道 | zhīdào | 20 |
| know (a person), recognize | 认识 認識 | rènshi | 12 |
| know how | 会 會 | huì | 26 |
| knowledge | 知识 知識 | zhīshi | 32 |
| Korea | 朝鲜 | Cháoxiǎn | 9 |
| labor (v.) | 劳动 勞動 | láodòng | 49 |
| laboratory | 实验室 實驗室 | shíyànshì | 15 |
| lack, short of | 差 | chà | 17 |
| lady, madam | 女士 | nǚshì | 9 |
| lady, madam, Mrs. | 夫人 | fūren | 27 |
| lake | 湖 | hú | 44 |
| lamp | 灯 燈 | dēng | 48 |
| lane | 胡同 | hútòng | 38 |
| language | 语言 語言 | yǔyán | 31 |
| Lantern Festival | 元宵节 元宵節 | Yuánxiāo Jié | 48 |
| lantern | 灯 燈 | dēng | 48 |
| lantern | 灯笼 燈籠 | dēnglong | 48 |
| last | 最后 最後 | zuìhòu | 50 |
| last (month, week) | 上(月，星期) | shàng (yuè, xīngqī) | 37 |
| last time | 上次 | shàngcì | 37 |
| last year | 去年 | qùnián | 30 |
| late | 晚 | wǎn | 25 |
| later on | 以后 以後 | yǐhòu | 17 |
| laugh | 笑 | xiào | 30 |

## English — 汉字 — Pinyin — Lesson

| English | 汉字 | Pinyin | Lesson |
|---|---|---|---|
| leaf | 叶子 | yèzi | 33 |
| lean, thin | 瘦 | shòu | 37 |
| leave | 离开 | líkāi | 29 |
| leave a message | 留言 | liú yán | 47 |
| leave for | 去 | qù | 12 |
| left (side) | 左(边) | zuǒ (biān) | 22 |
| leg | 腿 | tuǐ | 45 |
| lend | 借 | jiè | 49 |
| length | 长短 | chángduǎn | 37 |
| lesson | 课 | kè | 17 |
| let off (firecrackers) | 放(爆竹) | fàng (bàozhú) | 34 |
| let; ask (to do...) | 让 | ràng | 19 |
| letter | 信 | xìn | 14 |
| liberate (v.) | 解放 | jiěfàng | 36 |
| library | 图书馆 | túshūguǎn | 15 |
| lie down (v.) | 躺 | tǎng | 46 |
| life | 生命 | shēngmìng | 32 |
| life; to live | 生活 | shēnghuó | 47 |
| light | 灯 | dēng | 48 |
| light | 亮 | liàng | 43 |
| like (to be like), resemble, take after | 像 | xiàng | 21 |
| like (v.) | 喜欢 | xǐhuan | 19 |
| like this | 这样 | zhèyàng | 32 |
| line | 队 | duì | 28 |
| line is busy/engaged (phone) | 占线 | zhàn xiàn | 23 |
| line up (v.) | 排队 | pái duì | 38 |
| lion | 狮子 | shīzi | 42 |
| listen (v.) | 听 | tīng | 19 |
| literature | 文学 | wénxué | 26 |
| little | 小 | xiǎo | 22 |

| English | 汉字 | Pinyin | Lesson |
|---|---|---|---|
| little bit | 一点儿 一點兒 | yìdiǎnr | 25 |
| little while | 一会儿 一會兒 | yíhuìr | 41 |
| little while | 一下儿 一下兒 | yíxiàr | 11 |
| live | 住 | zhù | 10 |
| live; get along | 过 過 | guò | 30 |
| liver | 肝 | gān | 32 |
| living | 活 | huó | 47 |
| living room | 客厅 客廳 | kètīng | 22 |
| local flavor/style | 风味 風味 | fēngwèi | 43 |
| long | 长 長 | cháng | 31 |
| look | 看 | kàn | 7 |
| look for; call on | 找 | zhǎo | 16 |
| loose-fitting, fat | 肥 | féi | 37 |
| lose | 丢 | diū | 41 |
| lose (a game) | 输 輸 | shū | 28 |
| loud voice; loudly | 大声 大聲 | dàshēng | 34 |
| love | 爱 愛 | ài | 45 |
| lovely | 可爱 可愛 | kě'ài | 45 |
| low voice | 小声 小聲 | xiǎoshēng | 28 |
| luggage | 行李 | xíngli | 28 |
| lunch | 午饭 午飯 | wǔfàn | 32 |
| lungs | 肺 | fèi | 27 |
| madam | 夫人 | fūren | 37 |
| made to order | 定作 | dìngzuò | 15 |
| magazine | 杂志 雜誌 | zázhì | 34 |
| mailbox | 信箱 | xìnxiāng | 35 |
| major | 专业 專業 | zhuānyè | 38 |
| make a line (v.) | 排队 排隊 | pái duì | 28 |
| make a telephone call | 打 | dǎ | 35 |
| make money, earn | 挣 | zhèng | 11 |
| make use of | 用 | yòng | 35 |
| make use of | 利用 | lìyòng | 35 |

| English | 汉字 | | Pinyin | Lesson |
|---|---|---|---|---|
| male | 男 | | nán | 13 |
| man | 男子 | | nánzǐ | 40 |
| man of letters | 文学家 | 文學家 | wénxuéjiā | 47 |
| manager, director | 经理 | 經理 | jīnglǐ | 14 |
| manner | 样子 | 樣子 | yàngzi | 45 |
| many | 多 | | duō | 21 |
| Mao Tai | 茅台酒 | | Máotáijiǔ | 27 |
| map | 地图 | 地圖 | dìtú | 7 |
| marble pillar | 华表 | 華表 | huábiǎo | 42 |
| marry | 结婚 | 結婚 | jié hūn | 20 |
| masses | 群众 | 羣衆 | qúnzhòng | 47 |
| master | 师傅 | 師傅 | shīfu | 43 |
| match | 赛 | 賽 | sài | 28 |
| material (sewing) | 料子 | | liàozi | 37 |
| may | 可以 | | kěyǐ | 26 |
| may I ask... | 请问 | 請問 | qǐngwèn... | 9 |
| meal | 饭 | 飯 | fàn | 18 |
| meaning | 意思 | | yìsi | 39 |
| measure (v.) | 量 | | liáng | 32 |
| medical department | 医科 | 醫科 | yīkē | 32 |
| medicine | 药 | 藥 | yào | 46 |
| meet each other(v.) | 见面 | | jiàn miàn | 29 |
| meet, see (v.) | 见 | 見 | jiàn | 29 |
| menu | 菜单 | 菜單 | càidān | 4 |
| meter | 米 | | mǐ | 37 |
| midwinter | 隆冬 | | lóngdōng | 33 |
| military attaché | 武官 | | wǔguān | 27 |
| milk | 牛奶 | | niúnǎi | 43 |
| mineral water | 矿泉水 | 礦泉水 | kuàngquánshuǐ | 25 |
| mirror | 镜子 | 鏡子 | jìngzi | 44 |
| miss | 小姐 | | xiǎojiě | 19 |
| missus, Mrs. | 夫人 | | fūren | 27 |



| English | 汉字 | | Pinyin | Lesson |
|---|---|---|---|---|
| mist | 雾 | 霧 | wù | 33 |
| mistake | 错误 | 錯誤 | cuòwù | 47 |
| mister, Mr. | 先生 | | xiānsheng | 12 |
| model | 典型 | | diǎnxíng | 42 |
| modern | 现代 | 現代 | xiàndài | 19 |
| modernization | 现代化 | | xiàndàihuà | 31 |
| money | 钱 | 錢 | qián | 35 |
| month | 月 | | yuè | 20 |
| morning | 上午 | | shàngwǔ | 18 |
| most | 最 | | zuì | 33 |
| mother | 母亲 | 母親 | mǔqin | 44 |
| mother, mom | 妈妈 | 媽媽 | māma | 4 |
| motorcycle | 摩托车 | 摩托車 | mótuōchē | 41 |
| mouth | 嘴 | | zuǐ | 32 |
| move (v.) | 动 | 動 | dòng | 42 |
| move, take away (v.) | 搬 | | bān | 42 |
| move, touch (emotions) (v.) | 感动 | 感動 | gǎndòng | 49 |
| movie | 电影 | 電影 | diànyǐng | 17 |
| movie theater | 电影院 | | diànyǐngyuàn | 17 |
| Mr. | 先生 | | xiānsheng | 12 |
| Mrs. | 夫人 | | fūrén | 27 |
| Mrs. | 太太 | | tàitai | 21 |
| music | 音乐 | 音樂 | yīnyuè | 19 |
| mutually; each other | 互相 | | hùxiāng | 15 |
| name | 名字 | | míngzi | 13 |
| native | 本地 | | běndì | 34 |
| near | 近 | | jìn | 44 |
| neat, tidy | 整齐 | 整齊 | zhěngqí | 48 |
| needle | 针 | 針 | zhēn | 46 |
| neighbor | 邻居 | 鄰居 | línjū | 39 |
| nervous, anxious (to feel ~) | 着急 | | zháo jí | 35 |

| English | 汉字 | 汉字 | Pinyin | Lesson |
|---|---|---|---|---|
| package | 包裹 | 包裹 | bāoguǒ | 34 |
| pagoda | 塔 | 塔 | tǎ | 44 |
| pain | 疼 | 疼 | téng | 46 |
| pair | 双 | 雙 | shuāng | 28 |
| pair | 对 | 對 | duì | 39 |
| pancake (deep fried) | 油饼 | 油餅 | yóubǐng | 43 |
| panda | 熊猫 | 熊貓 | xióngmāo | 45 |
| panda exhibition hall | 熊猫馆 | 熊貓館 | xióngmāoguǎn | 45 |
| pants | 裤子 | 褲子 | kùzi | 16 |
| paper | 纸 | 紙 | zhǐ | 13 |
| parcel | 包裹 | 包裹 | bāoguǒ | 34 |
| park | 公园 | 公園 | gōngyuán | 33 |
| parking lot (bike) | 存车处 | 存車處 | cúnchēchù | 43 |
| parking lot (car) | 停车场 | 停車場 | tíngchēchǎng | |
| parlor | 客厅 | 客廳 | kètīng | 22 |
| part (v.) | 分别 | 分別 | fēnbié | 29 |
| participate | 参加 | 參加 | cānjiā | 20 |
| pass away (v.) | 逝世 | 逝世 | shìshì | 50 |
| passport | 护照 | 護照 | hùzhào | 31 |
| paste (v.) | 贴 | 貼 | tiē | 48 |
| patient | 病人 | 病人 | bìngrén | 46 |
| pavilion | 亭子 | 亭子 | tíngzi | 41 |
| pay (money) | 交 | 交 | jiāo | 37 |
| pay attention | 注意 | 注意 | zhùyì | 29 |
| pea gruel | 豌豆粥 | 豌豆粥 | wāndòuzhōu | 43 |
| peasant | 农民 | 農民 | nóngmín | 24 |
| pen | 笔 | 筆 | bǐ | 13 |
| people | 群众 | 群眾 | qúnzhòng | 47 |
| people | 人民 | 人民 | rénmín | 26 |
| perform (v.) | 演 | 演 | yǎn | 37 |
| perform, performance | 演出 | 演出 | yǎnchū | 49 |
| person | 人 | 人 | rén | 6 |

| English | 汉字 | 汉字 | Pinyin | Lesson |
|---|---|---|---|---|
| pharmacist | 药剂士 | 藥劑師 | yàojìshì | 46 |
| phone (v.) | 打电话 | 打電話 | dǎdiànhuà | 28 |
| photo, picture | 照片 | 照片 | zhàopiàn | 23 |
| physical training, exercise | 锻炼 | 鍛煉 | duànliàn | 24 |
| pictorial | 画报 | 畫報 | huàbào | 11 |
| picture | 图片 | 圖片 | túpiàn | 34 |
| picture, painting | 画儿 | 畫兒 | huàr | 36 |
| picture, photo | 照片 | 照片 | zhàopiàn | 23 |
| piece | 块 | 塊 | kuài | 23 |
| place | 地方 | 地方 | dìfang | 32 |
| place (v.) | 放 | 放 | fàng | 34 |
| plane | 飞机 | 飛機 | fēijī | 29 |
| plant, grow (v.) | 种 | 種 | zhòng | 46 |
| plate | 牌子 | 牌子 | páizi | 34 |
| platform | 主席台 | 主席台 | zhǔxítái | 40 |
| play | 打 | 打 | dǎ | |
| play (stringed instrument) | 拉 | 拉 | lā | 31 |
| play (v.) | 玩儿 | 玩兒 | wánr | 23 |
| please | 请 | 請 | qǐng | 8 |
| plum blossom | 梅花 | 梅花 | méihuā | 33 |
| pneumonia | 肺炎 | 肺炎 | fèiyán | 32 |
| poem | 诗 | 詩 | shī | 33 |
| poem | 诗歌 | 詩歌 | shīgē | 26 |
| point at (v.) | 指 | 指 | zhǐ | 34 |
| polite | 客气 | 客氣 | kèqi | 8 |
| popsicle | 冰棍儿 | 冰棍兒 | bīnggùnr | 42 |
| porcelain | 瓷器 | 瓷器 | cíqì | 36 |
| porridge, gruel | 粥 | 粥 | zhōu | 43 |
| possibly, probably | 可能 | 可能 | kěnéng | 46 |
| post office | 邮局 | 郵局 | yóujú | 34 |
| post office box | 信箱 | 信箱 | xìnxiāng | 34 |

## Page 29

| English | 汉字 | Pinyin | Lesson |
|---|---|---|---|
| postcard | 明信片 | míngxìnpiàn | 34 |
| precious, valuable | 珍贵 (珍貴) | zhēnguì | 45 |
| premier | 总理 (總理) | zǒnglǐ | 50 |
| prepare (v.) | 准备 (準備) | zhǔnbèi | 25 |
| prescription | 药方 (藥方) | yàofāng | 46 |
| present (n.) | 礼物 (禮物) | lǐwù | 48 |
| pretty, beautiful | 漂亮 | piàoliang | 21 |
| previous (occasion) | 上(次) | shàng (cì) | 37 |
| price | 价钱 (價錢) | jiàqián | 36 |
| probably | 可能 | kěnéng | 46 |
| procedure | 手续 (手續) | shǒuxù | 31 |
| produce (v.) | 生产 (生產) | shēngchǎn | 36 |
| professor | 教授 | jiàoshòu | 13 |
| program, item | 节目 (節目) | jiémù | 49 |
| progress, advance | 进步 (進步) | jìnbù | 29 |
| proverb | 成语 (成語) | chéngyǔ | 26 |
| public | 公共 | gōnggòng | 38 |
| pupil | 小学生 (小學生) | xiǎoxuéshēng | 27 |
| push | 推 | tuī | 43 |
| put | 放 | fàng | 34 |
| put in order | 收拾 | shōushi | 48 |
| put in order, arrange | 整理 | zhěnglǐ | 22 |
| put on a show | 演出 | yǎnchū | 49 |
| put on, wear (clothes) | 穿 | chuān | 16 |
| put up, hang (v.) | 挂 (掛) | guà | 34 |
| put, lay (the table) (v.) | 摆 (擺) | bǎi | 48 |
| quality | 质量 (質量) | zhìliang | 36 |
| question | 问题 (問題) | wèntí | 18 |
| queue up | 排队 (排隊) | páiduì | 38 |
| quick | 快 | kuài | 25 |
| rabbit | 兔子 | tùzi | 48 |

## Page 30

| English | 汉字 | Pinyin | Lesson |
|---|---|---|---|
| radio | 收音机 (收音機) | shōuyīnjī | 34 |
| radio announcer | 广播员 (廣播員) | guǎngbōyuán | 41 |
| rain (v.) | 下雨 | xiàyǔ | 33 |
| raincoat | 雨衣 | yǔyī | 37 |
| read | 看 | kàn | 7 |
| read aloud (v.) | 念 | niàn | 24 |
| reading room | 阅览室 (閱覽室) | yuèlǎnshì | 15 |
| realize (v.) | 实现 (實現) | shíxiàn | 31 |
| really, truly | 真 | zhēn | 21 |
| receipt | 收据 (收據) | shōujù | 34 |
| receive (v) | 收 | shōu | 34 |
| recently | 最近 | zuìjìn | 32 |
| reception | 招待会 (招待會) | zhāodàihuì | 27 |
| recognize (person, word) | 认识 (認識) | rènshi | 12 |
| record (n.) | 唱片 | chàngpiàn | 19 |
| record (v.) | 记录 (記錄) | jìlù | 40 |
| record (v.), recording | 录音 (錄音) | lùyīn | 46 |
| recover (v.) | 恢复 (恢復) | huīfù | 47 |
| red | 红 (紅) | hóng | 19 |
| red autumnal leaves | 红叶 (紅葉) | hóngyè | 33 |
| red lotus | 红莲 (紅蓮) | hónglián | 50 |
| referee, umpire | 裁判 | cáipàn | 28 |
| refreshments | 小吃 | xiǎochī | 43 |
| refreshments | 点心 (點心) | diǎnxīn | 24 |
| regard as (v.), to take somebody for | 作 | zuò | 47 |
| register (letter, in hospital) | 挂号 (掛號) | guà hào | 34 |
| regisration card | 挂号证 (掛號證) | guàhàozhèng | 46 |
| regular | 正常 | zhèngcháng | 32 |
| regular mail | 平信 | píngxìn | 34 |
| relax | 放心 | fàngxīn | 29 |

| English | 汉字 | Pinyin | Lesson |
|---|---|---|---|
| Shanghai | 上海 | Shànghǎi | 31 |
| she | 她 | tā | 5 |
| shirt, blouse | 襯衫 | chènshān | 16 |
| shoes | 鞋 | xié | 28 |
| shop | 店 | diàn | 43 |
| shop | 商店 | shāngdiàn | 13 |
| shop assistant | 售貨員 | shòuhuòyuán | 36 |
| shopkeeper | 掌櫃 | zhǎngguì | 49 |
| short | 短 | duǎn | 37 |
| short note | 條子 | tiáozi | 39 |
| short of, lacking | 差 | chà | 17 |
| should | 应该 | yīnggāi | 26 |
| shout (v.) | 喊 | hǎn | 44 |
| show (n.) | 演出 | yǎnchū | 49 |
| shut, close (v.) | 关 | guān | 46 |
| side | 边 | biān | 44 |
| side | 旁边 | pángbiān | 22 |
| sign (n.) | 迹 | jī | 33 |
| sign; plate | 牌子 | páizi | 34 |
| silk | 綢子(字) | chóu(zi) | 37 |
| simple, unadorned | 简朴 | jiǎnpǔ | 47 |
| sing (v.) | 唱 | chàng | 19 |
| sister (elder) | 姐姐 | jiějie | 14 |
| sister (younger) | 妹妹 | mèimei | 14 |
| sit (v.) | 坐 | zuò | 10 |
| situation | 情况 | qíngkuàng | 35 |
| six | 六 | liù | 11 |
| ski (v.), skiing | 滑雪 | huá xuě | 28 |
| skirt | 裙子 | qúnzi | 16 |
| sky | 天 | tiān | 44 |
| sleep (v.) | 睡觉 | shuì jiào | 18 |
| slow | 慢 | màn | 35 |

| English | 汉字 | Pinyin | Lesson |
|---|---|---|---|
| smart | 聰明 聪明 | cōngming | 39 |
| smile | 微笑 | wēixiào | 50 |
| smile (v.) | 笑 | xiào | 30 |
| smoke | 吸烟 | xī yān | 8 |
| snack | 點心 点心 | diǎnxīn | 24 |
| snack | 小吃 | xiǎochī | 43 |
| snackbar | 小吃店 | xiǎochīdiàn | 43 |
| snow | 雪 | xuě | 33 |
| so; such | 这么 | zhème | 42 |
| so; such; like this | 这样 | zhèyàng | 32 |
| soccer | 足球 | zúqiú | 28 |
| socialism | 社会主义 社會主義 | shèhuìzhǔyì | 31 |
| society | 社会 社會 | shèhuì | 49 |
| socks | 袜子 襪子 | wàzi | 37 |
| softly (speak ~) | 小声 小聲 | xiǎoshēng | 28 |
| solo (singing) | 独唱 獨唱 | dúchàng | 49 |
| some | 有的 | yǒude | 34 |
| sometimes | 有时候 有時候 | yǒu shíhou | 18 |
| son | 儿子 兒子 | érzi | 48 |
| soprano | 女高音 | nǚgāoyīn | 49 |
| sore | 疼 | téng | 46 |
| sorry | 对不起 對不起 | duìbuqǐ | 41 |
| soup | 汤 湯 | tāng | 25 |
| South America | 南美洲 | Nán Měi Zhōu | 7 |
| South Asia | 南亚 南亞 | Nán Yà | 45 |
| south (side) | 南(边) 南(邊) | nán(biān) | 38 |
| speak (v.) | 说 説 | shuō | 13 |
| speak (v.) | 讲 講 | jiǎng | 38 |
| specialty; major | 专业 專業 | zhuānyè | 35 |
| spectator; audience | 观众 觀衆 | guānzhòng | 40 |
| spend money (v.) | 花 | huā | 37 |

| English | 汉字 | | Pinyin | Lesson |
|---|---|---|---|---|
| swim | 游泳 | | yóuyǒng | 25 |
| synopsis | 说明书 | 說明書 | shuōmíngshū | 49 |
| table | 桌子 | | zhuōzi | 22 |
| table tennis | 乒乓球 | | pīngpāngqiú | 28 |
| tablet | 片 | | piàn | 46 |
| tackle (v.) | 办 | 辦 | bàn | 28 |
| tail | 尾巴 | | wěiba | 47 |
| take a bath (v.) | 洗澡 | | xǐzǎo | 22 |
| take after | 象 | 像 | xiàng | 21 |
| take away | 搬 | | bān | 42 |
| take care (v.) | 当心 | 當心 | dāngxīn | 43 |
| take off (v.) | 起飞 | 起飛 | qǐfēi | 29 |
| take someone as | 作 | | zuò | 47 |
| talk | 话 | 話 | huà | 31 |
| talk | 谈 | 談 | tán | 26 |
| tall | 高 | | gāo | 37 |
| tape recorder | 录音机 | 錄音機 | lùyīnjī | 46 |
| taste | 尝 | 嚐 | cháng | 27 |
| tasty | 好吃 | | hǎochī | 21 |
| taxi | 出租汽车 | 車 | chūzū qìchē | 38 |
| tea | 茶 | | chá | 8 |
| tea (scented) | 花茶 | | huāchá | 19 |
| teach (v.) | 教 | | jiāo | 15 |
| teacher | 老师 | 老師 | lǎoshī | 6 |
| teacup | 茶碗 | | cháwǎn | 36 |
| teahouse | 茶馆 | 茶館 | cháguǎn | 49 |
| team | 队 | 隊 | duì | 28 |
| teapot | 茶壶 | 茶壺 | cháhú | 36 |
| teaset | 茶具 | | chájù | 36 |
| telegram | 电报 | 電報 | diànbào | 34 |
| telephone | 电话 | 電話 | diànhuà | 23 |

| English | 汉字 | | Pinyin | Lesson |
|---|---|---|---|---|
| telephone switchboard; central unit | 总机 | 總機 | zǒngjī | 23 |
| television | 电视 | 電視 | diànshì | 23 |
| tell (v.) | 告诉 | 告訴 | gàosu | 14 |
| tell, speak (v.) | 讲 | 講 | jiǎng | 38 |
| temperature (body) | 体温 | 體溫 | tǐwēn | 46 |
| ten | 十 | | shí | 11 |
| ten thousand | 万 | 萬 | wàn | 42 |
| term (school) | 学期 | 學期 | xuéqī | 35 |
| terminal (bus) | 终点 | 終點 | zhōngdiǎn | 33 |
| terrible | 厉害 | 厲害 | lìhài | 46 |
| test (v.) | 考 | | kǎo | 35 |
| test, examination | 考试 | 考試 | kǎoshì | 35 |
| text | 课文 | 課文 | kèwén | 23 |
| than (preposition) | 比 | | bǐ | 28 |
| thank | 感谢 | | gǎnxiè | 21 |
| thank you | 谢谢你 | 謝謝你 | xièxie nǐ | 8 |
| that | 那 | | nà | 5 |
| theatre | 剧场 | 劇場 | jùchǎng | 49 |
| them | 他们 | 他們 | tāmen | 12 |
| there | 那儿 | | nàr | 15 |
| there is no need to | 不用 | | bù yòng | 31 |
| therefore | 所以 | | suǒyǐ | 29 |
| they; them (men) | 他们 | 他們 | tāmen | 12 |
| they; them (women) | 她们 | 她們 | tāmen | 3 |
| thick | 厚 | | hòu | 36 |
| thin | 薄 | | báo | 36 |
| thin, skinny | 瘦 | | shòu | 37 |
| thing | 东西 | 東西 | dōngxi | 30 |
| things, affairs | 事儿 | 事兒 | shìr | 17 |
| think of | 怀念 | 懷念 | huáiniàn | 47 |
| think, feel | 觉得 | 覺得 | juéde | 33 |

| English | 汉字 | Pinyin | Lesson |
|---|---|---|---|
| thirsty | 渴 | kě | 43 |
| this | 这 / 這 | zhè | 4 |
| this year | 今年 | jīnnián | 20 |
| thoughtful | 周到 | zhōudào | 41 |
| thousand | 千 | qiān | 42 |
| three | 三 | sān | 10 |
| ticket | 票 | piào | 16 |
| ticket office | 售票处 | shòupiàochù | 41 |
| ticket seller | 售票员 | shòupiàoyuán | 38 |
| tidy, neat | 整齐 | zhěngqí | 48 |
| tiger | 老虎 | lǎohǔ | 47 |
| tight | 瘦 | shòu | 37 |
| time (length) | 时间 / 時間 | shíjiān | 31 |
| time (when) | 时候 / 時候 | shíhou | 18 |
| tired (to feel) | 累 | lèi | 43 |
| to (a place) | 往 | wǎng | 38 |
| to, for | 对 / 對 | duì | 39 |
| toast (drink) | 干杯 / 乾杯 | gān bēi | 27 |
| today | 今天 | jīntiān | 20 |
| tofu, bean curd | 豆腐 | dòufu | 42 |
| together | 一起 | yìqǐ | 17 |
| toilet | 厕所 | cèsuǒ | 10 |
| tomorrow | 明天 | míngtiān | 23 |
| too much | 太 | tài | 16 |
| top | 上(边) | shàng(biān) | 22 |
| touch (feelings) | 感动 / 感動 | gǎndòng | 49 |
| toward (preposition) | 往 | wǎng | 38 |
| trace; track; sign | 迹 | jì | 33 |
| trade | 贸易 | màoyì | 44 |
| traffic signal or light | 红绿灯 / 紅綠燈 | hónglùdēng | 38 |
| train | 火车 / 火車 | huǒchē | 24 |
| trainer | 教练 / 教練 | jiàoliàn | 25 |

| English | 汉字 | Pinyin | Lesson |
|---|---|---|---|
| translate | 翻译 / 翻譯 | fānyì | 26 |
| translator | 翻译 | fānyì | 26 |
| travel (v.) | 旅行 | lǚxíng | 44 |
| tree | 树 / 樹 | shù | 33 |
| trolley | 电车 / 電車 | diànchē | 28 |
| troublesome, bothersome | 麻烦 | máfan | 48 |
| trousers | 裤子 / 褲子 | kùzi | 16 |
| truly | 真 | zhēn | 21 |
| try (v.) | 试 | shì | 27 |
| turn a corner (v.) | 拐弯 / 拐彎 | guǎiwān | 38 |
| two | 二 | èr | 10 |
| two (with measure word) | 俩 / 倆 | liǎ | 26 |
| two | 两 / 兩 | liǎng | 16 |
| type (m.w.) | 种 / 種 | zhǒng | 36 |
| typical, model | 典型 | diǎnxíng | 42 |
| umbrella | 雨伞 / 雨傘 | yǔsǎn | 11 |
| umpire | 裁判 | cáipàn | 28 |
| unadorned | 简朴 | jiǎnpǔ | 47 |
| unbiased, fair | 公平 | gōngpíng | 28 |
| uncle (older) | 大爷 | dàye | 38 |
| uncle (younger) | 叔叔 | shūshu | 39 |
| understand (v.) | 懂 | dǒng | 24 |
| understand (v.) | 了解 | liǎojiě | 26 |
| United States | 美国 / 美國 | Měiguó | 31 |
| university | 大学 | dàxué | 31 |
| untie | 解 | jiě | 46 |
| use, make use of | 利用 | lìyòng | 35 |
| use, make use of | 用 | yòng | 11 |
| used to | 习惯 | xíguàn | 33 |
| vacation | 度假 | dùjià | 44 |
| valuable | 珍贵 | zhēnguì | 45 |

| English | 汉字 | | Pinyin | Lesson |
|---|---|---|---|---|
| wool sweater | 毛衣 | | máoyī | 37 |
| word | 词 | 詞 | cí | 24 |
| word, character | 字 | | zì | 15 |
| words; talk | 话 | 語 | huà | 31 |
| work (v.) | 工作 | | gōngzuò | 14 |
| work; do | 干 | 幹 | gàn | 42 |
| work; job | 活儿 | 活兒 | huór | 42 |
| work; labor | 劳动 | 勞動 | láodòng | 49 |
| worker | 工人 | | gōngrén | 23 |
| works | 作品 | | zuòpǐn | 49 |
| workshop | 车间 | 車間 | chējiān | 39 |
| world | 世界 | | shìjiè | 50 |
| wrap | 包 | | bāo | 46 |
| write | 写 | 寫 | xiě | 14 |
| writer | 文学家 | 文學家 | wénxuéjiā | 47 |
| writer | 作家 | | zuòjiā | 26 |
| writings | 文章 | | wénzhāng | 47 |
| wrong | 错 | 錯 | cuò | 38 |
| year | 年 | | nián | 20 |
| year (this ~) | 今年 | | jīnnián | 20 |
| yesterday | 昨天 | | zuótiān | 28 |
| yield | 屈服 | | qūfu | 33 |
| you | 你 | | nǐ | 1 |
| you (polite) | 您 | | nín | 8 |
| young | 年轻 | 年輕 | niánqīng | 21 |
| young lady | 小姐 | | xiǎojiě | 19 |
| younger brother | 弟弟 | | dìdi | 3 |
| youth | 青年 | | qīngnián | 47 |
| zero | ○，零 | | líng | 10 |
| zoo | 动物园 | 動物園 | dòngwùyuán | 45 |